1970

	Final Reports Census tracts	Notes	Volume I Part A	Part 1 U.S. Sec 1	Sec 2	Parts 2–58 States	Volume II Part 1	Part 2	Part 3	Part 4	Part 5	Part 6	Part 7	Part 8	Part 9	Part 10	Final Reports Census tracts	Gen. dem. trends	Employment profiles	Notes
Demographic Characteristics																				
Aggregate population	•	•	•	•		•	•	•	•	•	•	•	•	•	•	•	•	•	•	•
Age	•	•		•		•	•	•	•	•	•	•	•	•	•	•	•	•	•	•
Race	•	•		•		•	•	•	•	•	•	•	•	•	•	•	•	•	•	•
Spanish origin	•			•		•	•	•	•	•	•	•	•	•	•	•	•			•
Sex	•			•		•	•	•	•	•	•	•	•	•	•	•			•	•
Marital status	•	•		•	•	•	•	•	•	•	•	•	•	•	•	•			•	•
Social and Economic Characteristics																				
Citizenship				•	•	•					•				•					•
Disabilities				•	•	•			•	•		•			•					•
Education	•	•		•	•	•	•	•	•	•		•	•	•	•	•	•		•	•
Employment/unemployment	•	•		•	•	•	•	•			•	•	•	•	•	•			•	•
Families	•	•		•	•	•	•	•	•	•		•	•	•	•	•	•		•	•
Farmers/farms					•				•	•			•							•
Fertility		•		•	•	•					•			•	•	•				•
Households	•	•		•	•	•	•	•	•	•		•		•	•	•				•
Housing	•			•			•	•		•		•		•	•		•	•	•	•
Immigration				•	•	•					•									
Income	•	•		•	•	•	•	•	•	•	•	•	•	•	•	•			•	•
Industry	•			•	•	•				•	•	•			•	•			•	•
Institutional population	•			•	•	•	•	•	•	•		•				•				
Labor force	•	•		•	•	•	•	•	•	•	•	•	•	•	•	•			•	•
Language				•			•	•	•						•	•				•
Migration/mobility	•	•		•	•	•	•	•	•	•	•	•	•		•	•	•	•	•	•
Military/veterans		•		•	•	•		•		•	•	•	•		•				•	•
Nativity	•	•		•	•	•	•	•	•	•				•	•	•			•	•
Occupations	•	•		•	•	•	•	•	•	•	•	•	•	•	•	•	•		•	•
Poverty		•		•	•	•	•	•	•			•	•	•	•				•	•
Transportation	•	•		•	•	•				•			•		•		•		•	•
Apportionment, Geography																				
Apportionment				•	•															•
Geography		•		•	•	•	•	•	•	•	•	•	•	•	•	•	•	•		•
Vital Statistics									•	•								•		•

Population Information in Twentieth Century Census Volumes : 1950-1980

by Suzanne Schulze

ORYX PRESS
1988

The rare Arabian Oryx is believed to have inspired the myth of the unicorn. This desert antelope became virtually extinct in the early 1960s. At that time several groups of international conservationists arranged to have 9 animals sent to the Phoenix Zoo to be the nucleus of a captive breeding herd. Today the Oryx population is nearly 800, and over 400 have been returned to reserves in the Middle East.

Copyright © 1988 by Suzanne Schulze
Published by The Oryx Press
2214 North Central at Encanto
Phoenix, Arizona 85004-1483

Published simultaneously in Canada.

Printed and Bound in the United States of America.

∞ The paper used in this publication meets the minimum requirements of American National Standard for Information Science—Permanence of Paper for Printed Library Materials, ANSI Z39.48, 1984.

Library of Congress Cataloging-in-Publication Data

Schulze, Suzanne.
    Population information in twentieth century census volumes.
1950–1980 / Suzanne Schulze.
        p.   cm.
    A guide to the U.S. Census Bureau's 1950–1980 decennial census volumes.
    ISBN 0-89774-400-4
    1. United States—Census—Indexes.   2. United States—Census, 17th, 1950—Indexes.   3. United States—Census, 18th, 1960—Indexes. 4. United States—Census, 19th, 1970—Indexes.   5. United States--Census, 20th, 1980—Indexes.   6. United States—Population--History—20th century—Sources—Indexes.   I. Title.
Z7164.D3S46 1988
[HA214]
304.6'0973—dc19   88–17937
                                                                  CIP

TABLE OF CONTENTS

GUIDE TO CENSUS VOLUMES FOR 1950, 1960 AND 1970   FRONT END PAGES

GUIDE TO CENSUS VOLUMES FOR 1980   BACK END PAGES

PREFACE AND ACKNOWLEDGMENTS v

HOW TO USE THIS BOOK vii

1950: POPULATION INFORMATION IN THE SEVENTEENTH DECENNIAL CENSUS 1

     VOLUME I   NUMBER OF INHABITANTS 4
     VOLUME II   CHARACTERISTICS OF THE POPULATION 8
     VOLUME III   CENSUS TRACT STATISTICS 17
     VOLUME IV   SPECIAL REPORTS 20
     NOTES ON OTHER 1950 CENSUS PUBLICATIONS WITH POPULATION INFORMATION . . . 35

1960: POPULATION INFORMATION IN THE EIGHTEENTH DECENNIAL CENSUS 41

     VOLUME I   CHARACTERISTICS OF THE POPULATION 45
     VOLUME II   SUBJECT REPORTS 61
     VOLUME III   SELECTED AREA REPORTS 85
     FINAL REPORTS 89
     NOTES ON OTHER 1960 CENSUS PUBLICATIONS WITH POPULATION INFORMATION . . . 92

1970: POPULATION INFORMATION IN THE NINETEENTH DECENNIAL CENSUS 99

     VOLUME I   CHARACTERISTICS OF THE POPULATION 103
     VOLUME II   SUBJECT REPORTS 125
     FINAL REPORTS 155
     NOTES ON OTHER 1970 CENSUS PUBLICATIONS WITH POPULATION INFORMATION . . 163

1980: POPULATION INFORMATION IN THE TWENTIETH DECENNIAL CENSUS 173

     VOLUME I   CHARACTERISTICS OF THE POPULATION 179
     VOLUME II   SUBJECT REPORTS 213
     SUPPLEMENTARY REPORTS 234
     ADVANCE REPORTS 278
     FINAL REPORTS 280
     NOTES ON OTHER 1980 CENSUS PUBLICATIONS WITH POPULATION INFORMATION . . 290

TERMINOLOGY USED IN THIS VOLUME 293

STATES AND OUTLYING AREAS IN 1950-1980 CENSUS VOLUMES 307

SUBJECTS OF QUESTIONNAIRE ITEMS ON 1950-1980 DECENNIAL CENSUSES 311

BIBLIOGRAPHY 312

AVAILABILITY OF CENSUS MATERIALS 316

PREFACE AND ACKNOWLEDGMENTS

This book, which serves as a guide to the 1950, 1960, 1970 and 1980 Decennial Censuses, is the third in a set of guides. The first two guides identify population information in the 1790 through 1890 and the 1900 through 1940 Censuses respectively.

The two earlier volumes were based on identification of census materials developed by Henry J. Dubester in his work as chief of the Census Library Project, a joint effort of the Bureau of the Census and the Library of Congress. Dubester completed his Catalog of United States Census Publications 1790-1940 in 1950, and his catalog has become a standard reference source for librarians searching for census materials. Dubester's Catalog is included, on distinguishable yellow pages, in the Census Bureau's 1974 publication Bureau of the Census Catalog of Publications, 1790-1972, a publication which is probably more readily available than Dubester's Catalog itself.

The earlier two guides in this set made use of Dubester's numbering system as an aid to identifying each census volume. Dubester's numbers appear at the top of the end-page charts to show each volume. In this third guide, the Census' own designation by volume or report number is used.

Beginning with 1940, many published census volumes include a table guide on their front pages. This book uses a similar system, but the table guides differ. I have made an effort to use the same terminology throughout the two hundred years of the census, although the actual terminology in published census volumes differs over that long period. At the end of this book, a chapter on terminology provides an explanation of each subject term used here.

The process for developing this guide was to go through each census volume page by page, and to match the subjects covered in each table with those already established in the two earlier guides. Surprisingly, the subjects have remained very much the same, and those listed on the end pages of this book are very nearly identical to those of the other two volumes. Fortunately, the need for the term "slavery" ended with the first guide; unfortunately, the term "paupers" in that volume has given way to "poverty" in the newest guide. "Religion," used as a subject in the first two guides, no longer appears, and "literacy" has given way to "education," which is used throughout the three guides in the set.

All of the data in the 1950-1980 Censuses come from the enumerations themselves; thus there are no foreign data as in some of the earlier volumes. There are very few data on vital statistics, a government function now taken over by other agencies.

vi

The National Foundation for the Humanities supported my work to develop the first guide in this set. Oryx Press published the results of that effort and suggested a second volume to cover the remaining period of Dubester's Catalog. This third guide now completes the set as a group of references covering the twenty decennial censuses of the nation's first two centuries.

There are dozens of opportunities for error on each page of this guide. I hope there are few and would welcome their being called to my attention, as they are my responsibility alone. In an effort to reduce their likelihood, I have asked a number of students at the University of Northern Colorado to take in hand the cited census volumes and try using the corresponding table guides. These students include Annette Jensen, Sarah Drohan, Gwen Reagor, Marc Major, Denise Rooman, Eric Rothaus and Amy Chandler. Their contribution should not go unmentioned.

Thanks are also due to Mary Alm and Theresa Solis of the Michener Library documents staff; to Tim Byrne and Marcia Meister, documents librarians at Norlin Library at the University of Colorado at Boulder, our regional depository library; and to Jerry O'Donnell of the Census Users Service Denver Regional Office. I also want to acknowledge the assistance of Mark Vanderhaar of the Congressional Information Service, publisher of the American Statistics Index; Margaret Bryzinski of the Greenwood Press; and Grace Waibel, long-time head of the Bureau of the Census Library at Suitland, Maryland.

I want to thank Carol Hunter, Magon Kinzie and Anne Thompson, editors at Oryx Press, and Linda Archer, who designed the end pages for this and the earlier volumes. The clarity of the end pages is essential to the usefulness of these guides. Also, I must thank Judieth Hillman, who corrected a near-final draft. And, of course, my husband, for having become a gourmet cook and for putting up with a messy home while I completed this guide. Thank you all!

Michener Library   Suzanne Schulze
University of Northern Colorado
Greeley
April 1988

HOW TO USE THIS BOOK

This book is designed to assist anyone searching for information about United States population in reports of the decennial censuses between 1950 and 1980. It is assumed that the searcher has no particular background in using the Census.

First, consult the table inside the covers. Note the subjects listed in the left-hand column. All population data are categorized here under those subjects. Next note the decennial years at the top of the table, and below them the volume numbers listed there. Volumes of the 1950, 1960 and 1970 Censuses are shown on the front end-pages, and those of the 1980 Census on the back end-pages.

Choose the subject which is the object of your search, and the decennial year in which you are interested. Information from the four censuses of 1950 through 1980 is included in this book. It should be noted, however, that many census volumes include data from earlier decennial years, as noted by the term "historic." This information has usually been included for comparative purposes, but often saves one the trouble of finding an earlier census volume which may not be so readily available. Information from decennial censuses for 1790 through 1940 is included in two earlier volumes of this set.

When you have chosen the subject, look across the table until you find a mark in the proper decennial year. Then note the volume listed at the top of the table. Turn to the first page for that volume in the book. This page gives identifying information and classification numbers for that volume. Then turn to its table guide and look for the subject you are searching. The subjects are listed in the same order as on the end-pages. At the end of the volumes listed for each decennial year, there is a column entitled "Notes." These shorter citations refer to less important census publications which do, however, include some population information and may include some materials on your subject.

One caution should be noted about the table guides. Most of these guides show the exact table numbers for the subject and the geographical areas for which the data are available. In the case of the subject reports, which give more cross classifications of data, and less geographical information, only an "x" is provided to show whether the demographic, social or economic characteristic is used at all. These reports are based on sample data. In 1950 they are entitled Special Reports, and in 1960, 1970 and 1980, they are entitled Subject Reports.

If you have not already done so, this might be the best time to consult a librarian to determine where census volumes are kept in the library you are using and what classification system is used for census volumes. Once you know this, note the classification of your needed volume, determine whether it is held in your library, and then look for the tables you need in that volume.

If your library does not have a paper copy, you may need to make use of a microform collection. Most of the census materials in this guide, if not all, are available in that format. If you need to use microfilm or microfiche, be sure to note the exact details from the table guide.

Be sure to check all the sources in your library before attempting to use interlibrary loan or visiting another library with a census collection. Some libraries will not lend census materials, but will copy requested tables. You may wish to copy some pages from this book to make searching easier. The union list at the end of this book is there as a convenience for librarians to note the holdings of other libraries, and it may assist you in deciding whether it would be useful to visit another collection.

Population Information in Twentieth Century Census Volumes : 1950-1980

REGIONS AND GEOGRAPHIC DIVISIONS OF THE UNITED STATES

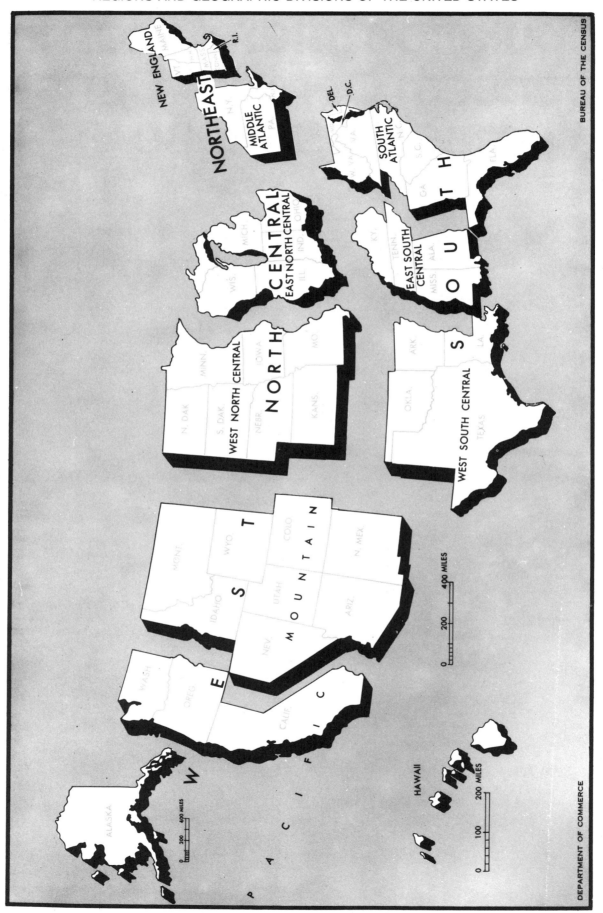

BUREAU OF THE CENSUS

DEPARTMENT OF COMMERCE

The 1940 Census established a pattern of two characteristics which
have since continued through each census: the separation of the population census from the housing census and the use of sampling procedures for many of the inquiries.

The enumeration of the population has, of course, continued as a
count of each individual. Certain questions are asked about every
person. Additional questions are asked of others. Throughout the
twentieth century, age, sex and race as well as marital status have
been asked of each respondent. The 1950 Census also obtained complete counts on other questions and two sizes of samples, 20 percent
and 3 1/3 percent. More information regarding the samples is given
below.

Major Population Reports

The 1950 Census broke little new ground. It was published in four
volumes, the first two distributed by the Census Bureau bound in
black, the other two in paper bindings. No consistency of appearance for the third and fourth volumes can therefore be expected among
libraries. In addition, the 1950 Census produced a number of unbound
separate reports.

Volume I, Number of Inhabitants, contains the population counts for
the United States, the 48 states, the District of Columbia and the
outlying possessions. These data had been published in the Series P-A
Bulletins. They also appears as Chapter A in each part of Volume II,
Characteristics of the Population. The latter, which has 54 separate parts, also contains the information in the Series P-B Bulletins,
with general social and economic characteristics, and the P-C Bulletins with detailed characteristics.

Volume III contains 64 separate parts, with data for Census Tracts.
These reports include data on both population and housing for those
cities of 50,000 which had been tracted. Data for each tract are similar to those found for the states in Volume II, though not as extensive. Volume IV includes the Special Reports. It appeared in five
groups of 20 parts, encompassing data compiled for economic characteristics, family characteristics, national origin and race, migration, education and fertility along with other data by size of place.

Unlike any other census, some of the findings in 1950 were published
by a publisher other than the U.S. government. Fourteen volumes in
the Census Monograph series were published between 1955 and 1958 by
Wiley through an arrangement with the Social Science Research Council.
These volumes were never given Superintendent of Documents classifica-

---

tion numbers and do not appear in the <u>Monthly Catalog</u>. They can be located through the National Union Catalog and other library reference sources.

The Census Bureau had been working throughout the decade of the forties on the development of improved computers for processing the huge masses of data. UNIVAC-I was put to use for the 1950 Census but was found not entirely successful, and experiments continued until FOSDIC was developed in time for the 1960 Census.

Population Inquiries

In 1950, enumeration of the population was still performed by visitors to each home who copied answers onto large sheets they carried. Each fourth and ninth line on the sheet was designated a "sample line," and additional information was requested for persons whose names happened to fall on that line, thus providing for a 20 percent sample. In addition, a 3 1/3 percent sample was taken for a few questions. When an enumerator found that a child had been born in the first three months of the year, that is, prior to April 1st, he was also to fill out an "infant card." Information compiled from these cards was compared with birth statistics in an effort to determine how well data corresponded with those from non-census records.

The standard questions of sex, age, race, marital status and relationship to the household head were listed on the 1950 form. However, the enumerator was instructed not to inquire as to race, but to determine race by observation, and to ask only in case of doubt. There were a number of other inquiries made on a 100 percent basis: place of birth and citizenship, and for those over 14 years, occupation and industry. For those whose names fell on the sample lines, the additional inquiries related to residence the year before, birth place of one's father and mother, highest grade of school attended, whether that grade was completed, and current school attendance. For those in the sample over age 14, there were questions about employment status, income, income of relatives if living in the household, veteran status and, if ever married, whether married more than once, and length of time in that marital status. For an ever-married woman there was a question as to how many children she had borne. Most of the data obtained in the 20 percent sample were published in Volume II with its 64 parts. The <u>Special Reports</u>, which comprise Volume IV, include data from the 3 1/3 percent sample.

1950
MAJOR POPULATION VOLUMES OF THE SEVENTEENTH DECENNIAL CENSUS

VOLUME	TITLE
Volume I	Number of Inhabitants
Volume II	Characteristics of the Population Part 1 - United States Summary Parts 2-54 - States, Territories and Possessions
Volume III	Census Tract Statistics Parts 1-64
Volume IV	Special Reports

Part 1   Economic Characteristics
  1 A Employment and Personal Characteristics
  1 B Occupational Characteristics
  1 C Occupation by Industry
  1 D Industrial Characteristics

Part 2   Family Characteristics
  2 A General Characteristics of Families
  2 B (Detailed Characteristics of Families was
      planned, but not issued)
  2 C Institutional Population
  2 D Marital Status
  2 E Duration of Current Marital Status

Part 3   National Origin and Race
  3 A Nativity and Parentage
  3 B Nonwhite Population by Race
  3 C Persons of Spanish Surname
  3 D Puerto Ricans in Continental United States

Part 4   Mobility of the Population
  4 A State of Birth
  4 B Population Mobility - States and State
      Economic Areas
  4 C Population Mobility - Farm and Nonfarm Movers
  4 D Population Mobility - Characteristics of
      Migrants

Part 5 A Characteristics by Size of Place
  5 B Education
  5 C Fertility

Notes on other publications of the 1950 Census that contain population information are provided at the end of the 1950 section.

Decennial Year	1950
Census	Seventeenth Decennial Census
Volume	Volume I
Title	Census of Population: 1950 Number of Inhabitants
Publication	Department of Commerce, Bureau of the Census Washington, DC: Government Printing Office
Date	1952

Classifications

Supt. of Documents	C 3.950-7/5:v.1
Library of Congress	HA 201.1950.A2 v.1
card	52-60089 rev.
Dewey	312.0973
University of Texas	1950.1

Microforms

Research Pubns.	Film 1950 Reel 1
Pages	xliii, 1,428 pages - separately numbered for each chapter, i.e., state or territory
Maps, illustrations	14 U.S. maps; counties, minor civil divisions, and urbanized areas for each state

Notes

This volume is a compilation of 54 P-A reports which were also separately published. The volume includes total population counts for each county, minor civil division, places of 1,000, and places of 5,000 by wards.

On the following pages there are separate table guides for the U.S. chapter and for Chapters 2-54 for states and territories. In addition to the District of Columbia, territories include Alaska, Hawaii, Puerto Rico, and the outlying possessions of American Samoa, the Canal Zone, Guam and the Virgin Islands. There are 33 tables in the U.S. chapter and 9 tables in the other chapters.

1950
Volume I   Number of Inhabitants

Chapter 1 United States Tables 1-33	United States	Regs., Divns.	States, Terrs.	Other
<u>Demographic Characteristics</u>				
Aggregate population	1	6	6	
Historic from 1790	2	6	6	
percent increase	7	7	7	
percent distribution	8	8	8	
Rank from 1900			11	
Rank by increase			12	
U.S. territories, possessions	1			
Population living abroad	1			
Standard Metropolitan Areas				26
constituent parts				26
historic from 1940				26,27
rank				28
population inside/outside central cities				27
population of 1940 Metro- politan Districts				30
Urbanized areas				17
rank				18
Counties				19
historic from 1940				19
percent change since 1940 by state				20
Cities of 100,000				23
historic from earliest census				23
rank of 50 largest				25
Urban places				24
historic from 1940				24
Economic Subregions				31
Special censuses 1940-1950				32

1950
Volume I Number of Inhabitants

Chapter 1 United States Tables 1-33	United States	Regs., Divns.	States, Terr.	Other
Apportionment, Geography				
Apportionment from 1790	10	10	10	
Density	9	9	9	
Historic from 1790	2			
from 1900	9	9	9	
Of metropolitan areas				29
Of urbanized areas				17
Number incorporated places by state				22
Number and type minor civil divisions by state				21
Number census tracts in tracted areas				33
Size of places	5a,16	16	16	
Historic from 1790	5b			
Urban/rural				
Composition of urban population	13	13	13	
Composition of urban and rural population	14	14	14	
Historic from earliest census	4		15	15
Urban areas under 1940 rules				3

1950
Volume I Number of Inhabitants

Chapters 2-54
States and Territories   Note that some states and territories have
Tables 1-9   less population and thus fewer tables.

	State	Counties	Places
Demographic Characteristics			
Aggregate population	1	5	4,7,8
Historic from earliest census	1		
Counties		5	
historic from earliest census		5	
Minor civil divisions		6	
historic from 1930		6	
Urban places			4
historic from earliest census			4
Cities of 5,000 or more, by wards			8
Incorporated places			7
historic from 1940			7
Unincorporated places of 1,000 or more			7
historic from 1940			7
Urbanized areas and constituent parts			9

Decennial Year   1950

Census   Seventeenth Decennial Census

Volume   Volume II   Part I

Title   Census of Population: 1950
                            Characteristics of the Population
                            Part I United States Summary

Publication   Department of Commerce, Bureau of the Census
                            Washington, DC: Government Printing Office

Date   1953

Classifications

   Supt. of Documents   C 3.950-7/5:v.2/pt.1

   Library ofCongress   HA 201.1950.A2 v.2 pt.1

      card   52-60089 rev.

   Dewey   312.0973

   University of Texas   1950.2

Microforms

   Research Pubns.   Films 1950   Reel 1

Pages   xii, 486 pages

Maps, illustrations   Numerous maps and figures

Notes   This volume includes three sections: Number
                            of Inhabitants, General Characteristics, and
                            Detailed Characteristics of the Population.
                            The sections correspond to Series P-A, P-B and
                            P-C, which were previously issued in paper
                            covers.

                            There is a lengthy introductory section of 66
                            pages, and a detailed table guide at the be-
                            ginning of the volume, and a copy of the 1950
                            questionnaire together with instructions to the
                            enumerators at the end.

1950
Volume II   Characteristics of the Population   Part 1   United States
Summary

	United States	Regs., Divns.	States, Terr.	Places
Demographic Characteristics				
Aggregate population	1,6	6	6	17
Historic from 1790	2,6	6	6	
from 1900			11,12	
Decennial increase	7	7	7	
Percent distribution	8	8	8	
Population abroad	1,35, 40,45			
Standard Metropolitan Areas				26-29,86
1940 Metropolitan Districts				30
Urbanized areas				17,93
Counties				19,20
Cities				23,25
Urban places				24
Economic Subregions				31
Areas with special censuses since 1940				32
Age	37	145,146		86,87,93
Historic from 1880	39,98			
By race and sex	61	61	61	
historic from 1940	38			
By sex		62	63	
Median age	64	64,167	64,167	177
Race	34-36, 59,61	59,61	59,61	93
White, Negro	36			
Indian, Japanese, Chinese	36			
Sex	34,60, 61	60,61	60,61	
Males per females				86
Marital status	45,68, 102,103	68,147, 168	68,168	178
Historic from 1890	46,102			
By presence of spouse	104-106	147		
Married couples	47,69	69	69	86

1950
Volume II   Characteristics of the Population   Part 1   United States
Summary

	United States	Regs., Divns.	States, Terr.	Places
Social and Economic Characteristics				
Citizenship	40			
Of population 21+ years	41,65,101			
Education				
School enrollment	42,43, 66,109-113,117	66, 150-152, 171	66,171	179,180
historic from 1910	43			
Years of school completed	44,67, 114-116	67,153, 154,170, 172,173	67,170, 172,173	86,93, 181
Employment/unemployment	50,52,72 118	72,155, 157	72	88,89,93
Hours worked census week	122,123, 135			
Class of employer	53			
Families	47	69	69	
Households	47,107	148,149		86
Persons per household		169		86,93
Quasi households	108	149		
Income	57,84,85, 129,136-144	84,85, 162-166, 175,176	84,85, 175,176	92,93, 185
Industry	55,80-83, 130	80-83, 160,161	80-83	91
Historic from 1940	56,131-136			
Institutional population	72,73,118	72,73	72,73	88
Labor force	5,17,120, 12,174	74,156, 174	74,174	88,89, 93,182, 183
Class of employer	54,75,129	75	75	90
In/not in, reason	72,73,118	72,73	72,73	88,89
By school enrollment				184

1950
Volume II   Characteristics of the Population   Part 1   United States Summary

	United States	Regs., Divns.	States, Terr.	Places
Migration/mobility				
Residence in 1949	48,70	70	70	86,93
Nativity				
General nativity	35,59,65, 94,96,97, 99,100	65	65	86
Specific by country of birth	49,71	71	71	
Occupations	53,76-79, 124,125	76-79, 158,159	76-79	90
Historic from 1940	125			
Apportionment, Geography				
Apportionment	10	10	10	
Historic from 1789	10	10	10	
Density	2,9	9	9	
History from 1790	2			
from 1900	9	9	9	
Of Standard Metropolitan Areas				29
Minor Civil Divisions				
Number and type			21	
Incorporated places				
Number and type			22	
Census tracts - number			33	
Size of place	5a	16	16	
Historic from 1900	5b			
Urban/rural	4,13,14 15	13,14,74	13,14,74	
Historic from earliest date	15			
By age and race	38,94,97	61,145		
By race and sex	34,36			
By marital status	104,105	147		
Citizenship and nativity	41			

1950
Volume II Characteristics of the Population Part 1 United States
Summary

	United States	Regs., Divns.	States, Terrs.	Places
Urban/rural (continued)				
Education				
school enrollment	42,109, 111,112, 117	151,152		
years of school completed	44,114, 115	154		
Employment	50,118, 119	155,157		
by class of employer	53			
by weeks worked	122			
Households	107,108	148,149		
Industry	57			
Income	138			
Labor force	74	74,156	74	
Migration/mobility	48,126			
Rural farm/nonfarm	74			

Decennial Year	1950
Census	Seventeenth Decennial Census
Volume	Volume II Parts 2 through 54
Title	Census of Population: 1950 Characteristics of the Population States, Territories and Possessions
Publication	Department of Commerce, Bureau of the Census Washington, DC: Government Printing Office
Date	1953 and 1954

Classifications

Supt. of Documents	C 3.950-7/5:v.2/pts.2-54
Library of Congress	HA 201.1950.A2 v.2 pts.2-54
card	52-60089 rev.
Dewey	312.0973
University of Texas	1950.2 through 1950.55

Microforms

Research Pubns.	Film 1950 Reels 1-13

Pages	Vary
Maps, illustrations	Map of counties, minor civil divisions, and urbanized areas for each state and territory.

Notes

This volume comprises series P-A, Number of Inhabitants; P-B, General Population Characteristics; and P-C, Detailed Population Characteristics, which were previously issued in paper covers. Parts 2-50 are reports for the 48 states and the District of Columbia; Parts 51-53 for Alaska, Hawaii, and Puerto Rico; and Part 54 for American Samoa, Canal Zone, Guam and the Virgin Islands.

A detailed table guide is found at the front of each part. A set of 1950 definitions follows, as well as a statement as to the sample sizes. There is also a list of the industrial classifications used in 1950.

1950
Volume II   Characteristics of the Population   Parts 2-54

	State	SMAs	Counties	Other
Demographic Characteristics				
Aggregate population	1,10	9,10	5,6,12, 41	4,7,8
Historic from earliest census	1			4
from 1930			56	
from 1940			41	7
Minor civil divisions			6	
Urban places				10,11, 34,38
urban farms				34
Urbanized areas		9,10,34		
Age				
Single years	51-53			
In 5-year groups	15	33,53, 54	41	38,40, 53
Median age	10	10	12	10,11
Historic from earliest census	16			
Percent 65+ years	10	10	12	10,11
Race	10	10	12	10,11
Historic from 1880	16			
By sex	13		41,42	38
Indian, Chinese, Japanese			47	47
Sex - Nearly all tables by sex	53	34	41,42	34,38, 40
Marital status				
Historic from 1890	56			
By race	21,22	34	42	38,57
By presence of spouse	57	57		
Married couples	22	34		34
Social and Economic Characteristics				
Citizenship	17	34	42	34
By age	55			55

1950
Volume II Characteristics of the Population Parts 2-54

	State	SMAs	Counties	Other
Education				
School enrollment	10,18, 19	10,34	12,42	10,34, 65
Years of school completed	10,64, 65	34,64, 65	48	11,34, 38,64, 65
Employment/unemployment	10,66	10,35,66		10,11, 35,39, 65
By age and sex	67	67		67
By race and sex	25,27			
nonwhites	35			
By class of employer	29			
Persons 14-29 years, by school enrollment	71	71		
Families	72	34	42	34
Farms	87	49		40
Urban farms				34
Households	22,58	34	42	34
Persons by relationship	59	59		
Persons per household	10	10	12	10
Married couples without own household	22	34	22,42	34
Income				
Families - median	10	10,37	12,45	10,11, 37
Families, unrelated individuals	32	37	46	37
Family income	90			
Persons by family status	78	78		
Type of income	93,94			
Industry	10,30	10	12,43	10,11, 39
Historic from 1940	31,80			
By employment status	79,85			
By class of employer	83			
Institutional population	22	34		34

1950
Volume II   Characteristics of the Population   Parts 2-54

	State	SMAs	Counties	Other
Labor force				
Number persons in labor force	10,69	10,35	12,43, 44,48	10,11, 35
Employment by race	25			
historic from 1940	26,69			
By class of employer	28			
By major occupation group	28			
Migration/mobility				
Percent in same house 1949	10	10	42	10
Residence in 1949	23	34	42	34
Nativity				
General nativity	17,34	34	43,48	38,40
By country of origin	24	34a	42a	34a
Occupations	73	73		73
Historic from 1940	74			
by age	76			
By race	77			
By class of employer	77			

Apportionment, Geography

	State	SMAs	Counties	Other
Geography - land area	5		5	
Size of place	2			
Historic from 1900	3			
Urban/rural	1			5
Age	15,52,53			
Race	13,14			
Sex	13,14			
Marital status	57			
Occupations	75			
Rural farm and nonfarm	10,13		48,49	

Decennial Year	1950
Census	Seventeenth Decennial Census
Volume	Volume III, Chapters 1 through 64
Title	Census Tract Statistics (City)
Publication	Department of Commerce, Bureau of the Census Washington, DC: Government Printing Office
Date	1951, 1952 and 1953

Classifications

Supt. of Documents	C 3.950-7/2:(State Cutter/City Cutter)
Library of Congress	HA 201.1950.A2 v.3
card	52-60089 rev.
Dewey	312.0973
University of Texas	1950.53 through 1950.116

Microforms

Research Pubns.	Film 1950 Reel 13
Pages	Vary
Maps, illustrations	Map of Census Tracts at end of tables
Notes	The 64 separately published chapters of this series were issued unbound as Bulletins P-D. They combine data on both population and housing for those cities which had been tracted and which had a population of 50,000. Each tract was designed to include between 3,000 and 6,000 persons of relatively homogenous characteristics.
	The P-D bulletins superseded earlier Series PC-10 reports. The following cities were not included in the P-D bulletins but had PC-10 reports: Atlantic City, Augusta, Des Moines, Macon, Savannah and those in northeastern New Jersey. There are but 5 tables in these reports, with two additional ones with data on the Spanish surnamed population in the 5 southwestern states.

1950
Volume III   Chapters 1-64   Census Tract Statistics

	City	Tracts*
Demographic Characteristics		
Aggregate population	1	1
Historic from 1940	1	1
Age		
Five year groups	2	2,6
By race - White and nonwhite	2	2
Persons 14 years and over	2	2,4,6
Persons 25+ years	1	1
nonwhite		4
Spanish surname		6
Race and Spanish surname		
White, nonwhite; Negro, other races	1	1
Historic from 1940 - White, nonwhite	1	1
Spanish surname		6
Sex	1	1,4,6
Marital status	2	2,4,6
Married couples	1	1,4
Social and Economic Characteristics		
Citizenship		6
Education		
Years of school completed	1	1,4,6
median years	1	1,4,6
Employment/unemployment	2	2,4,6
By sex		4,6
Families		
Families and unrelated individuals	1	1

*Tables 4 and 5 are included only where there are 250+ nonwhites in
 the tract. Tables 6 and 7 are included only where there are 250+
 Spanish surnamed persons in the tract and are only included for 5
 southwestern states.

1950
Volume III   Chapters 1-64   Census Tract Statistics

	City	Tracts
Households		
Number households	1	1
Population of households	1	1
Persons per household	1	1
Married couples with/without households	1	1,4
Housing		
Number dwelling units	3	3,5,7
Tenancy by race	3	3,5
Number persons in unit	3	3,5,7
Persons per room	3	3,5,7
Income and property		
Income of family & unrelated individuals	1	1,4
Median income	1	1,4
Institutional population	1	1
Labor force	2	2,4,6
Migration		
Residence in 1949	1	1,4
Nativity		
General nativity	1	1,6
Country of birth of foreign born Whites	1	1
Born in Mexico, other countries		6
Occupations	2	2,4
By sex		4

Volume IV Special Reports

Decennial Year   1950

Census   Seventeenth Decennial Census

Volume   Volume IV Special Reports Part 1

Title   Economic Characteristics
                            Part 1 A   Employment and Personal Character-
                                       istics
                            Part 1 B   Occupational Characteristics
                            Part 1 C   Occupation by Industry
                            Part 1 D   Industrial Characteristics

Publication   Department of Commerce, Bureau of the Census
                            Washington, DC: Government Printing Office

  Date   1 A 1953, 1 B 1956, 1 C 1954, 1 D 1955

Classifications

  Supt. of Documents   C 3.950-7/6:pts.1 A, B, C, D

  Library of Congress   HA 201.1950.A2 v.iv pts.1 A, B, C, D

    card   52-60089 rev.

  Dewey   312.0973

  University of Texas   1950.117 through 1950.120

Microforms

  Research Pubns.   Film 1950 Reel 16

Pages   1 A, 143 pages; 1 B, 266 pages; 1 C, 79 pages;
                            1 D, 86 pages

Maps, illustrations   Part A, 2 figures

Notes   Information in these reports is based on a
                            3 1/3 percent sample.

                            Parts 1 A, B and D provide considerable
                            demographic as well as social and economic
                            data, but 1 C is restricted to occupational
                            data by sex and by industry.

1950
Volume IV Special Reports Parts 1 A, B, C and D

	Part A	Part B	Part C	Part D
Demographic Characteristics				
Total persons age 14 and over	x			
Age	x	x		x
Race	x	x		x
Sex	x	x	x	x
Marital status	x	x		
Social and Economic Characteristics				
Citizenship		x		
Education				
School enrollment, persons 14 to 29	x	x		
Years school completed		x		
Employment/unemployment				
Persons employed	x	x	x	x
Persons unemployed	x			
By class of employer		x		x
By hours worked census week	x	x		x
By weeks worked 1949	x	x		x
Households	x			
Income		x		x
Wage and salary income		x		x
Industry			x	x
Detailed industry				x
Labor force	x	x		x
Persons not in labor force	x			
Migration/mobility		x		
Nativity	x			

1950
Volume IV Special Reports Parts 1 A, B, C and D

	Part A	Part B	Part C	Part D
Occupation	x	x		x
Detailed occupation		x	x	
<u>Apportionment, Geography</u>				
Size of place	x			
Urban/rural	x	x		x
Rural farm/nonfarm	x	x		x

Decennial Year	1950
Census	Seventeenth Decennial Census
Volume	Volume IV Special Reports Part 2
Title	Family Characteristics Part 2 A General Characteristics of Families Part 2 C Institutional Population Part 2 D Marital Status Part 2 E Duration of Current Marital Status
Publication	Department of Commerce, Bureau of the Census Washington, DC: Government Printing Office
Date	2 A and E 1955, 2 C and D 1953
Classifications	
Supt. of Documents	C 3.950-7/6:pts.2 A, C, D, E
Library of Congress	HA 201.1950.A23 v.4 pts.2 A, C, D, E
card	52-60089 rev.
Dewey	312.0973
University of Texas	1950.121, 1950.123 through 1950.125
Microforms	
Research Pubns.	Film 1950 Reel 16
Pages	2 A, iv, 225; 2 C, iv, 211; 2 D, iv, 64; 2 E iv, 51 pages
Maps, illustrations	Part 2 A, 2 maps
Notes	Information in 2 A is based on a special sample, as is 2 E; 2 C and D are based on a 3 1/3 percent sample. Each of the four parts has demographic as well as socioeconomic characteristic data. Part 2 B, Detailed Characteristics of Families, was planned but never published.

1950
Volume IV   Special Reports   Parts 2 A, C, D and E

	Part A	Part C	Part D	Part E
Demographic Characteristics				
Aggregate population		x		
Age	x	x	x	x
Of family head, wife, children	x			
Persons 14 years and over			x	
Persons 15-59 years				x
Race	x	x	x	x
Sex	x	x	x	x
Marital status	x	x	x	x
Social and Economic Characteristics				
Citizenship		x		
Education				
School enrollment		x		
Years of school completed	x	x		x
Employment/unemployment	x			
Families	x		x	
Farmers, farms		x	x	x
Fertility				x
Households			x	
Income	x	x	x	
Industry	x			
Institutional population		x		
Labor force	x			x
Migration/mobility	x	x		x

1950
Volume IV   Special Reports   Parts 2 A, C, D and E

	Part A	Part C	Part D	Part E
Nativity		x		
Occupations	x			
Apportionment, Geography				
Regions	x	x		
States	x	x		
Standard Metropolitan Areas	x	x		
Large cities	x	x		
Size of place	x			
Regions	x	x		
Urban/rural	x		x	x
Farm/nonfarm	x	x	x	x
Vital Statistics				
Marriages				x

Decennial Year	1950

Census   Seventeenth Decennial Census

Volume   Volume IV Special Reports Part 3

Title   National Origin and Race
Part 3 A   Nativity and Parentage
Part 3 B   Nonwhite Population by Race
Part 3 C   Persons of Spanish Surname
Part 3 D   Puerto Ricans in Continental
            United States

Publication   Department of Commerce, Bureau of the Census
Washington, DC: Government Printing Office

Date   3 A 1954; 3 B, C and D 1953

Classifications

Supt. of Documents   C 3.950-7/6:pts.3 A, B, C, D

Library of Congress   HA 201.1950.A2. v.4 pts.3 A, B, C and D

   card   52-60089 rev.

Dewey   312.0973

University of Texas   1950.126 through 1950.129

Microforms

Research Pubns.   Film 1950 Reel 16

Pages   3 A iv, 296; 3 B iv, 88; 3 C iv, 70; 3 D
iv, 18 pages

Maps, illustrations Few maps

Notes   Information in these reports is based on a
20 percent sample.

Each part in this series provides demographic
as well as social and economic characteristics
of the reported population groups.

1950
Volume IV   Special Reports   Parts 3 A, B, C and D

	Part A	Part B	Part C	Part D
Demographic Characteristics				
Aggregate population	x	x		
Total nonwhites		x		
Total Puerto Ricans in continental U.S.				x
Age	x	x	x	x
Race	x	x	x	x
White	x			
Negro		x		
Indian		x		
Japanese		x		
Chinese		x		
Filipino		x		
All other		x		
Sex	x	x	x	x
Marital status	x	x	x	x
Spanish surname				
Whites only; limited to five southwestern states: Arizona, California, Colorado, New Mexico and Texas	x		x	
Social and Economic Characteristics				
Citizenship	x	x	x	
Education				
School attendance	x			
Years of school completed	x	x	x	x
Employment/unemployment		x	x	x
Housing			x	
Income		x	x	x
Labor force		x	x	x

1950
Volume IV Special Reports Parts 3 A, B, C and D

	Part A	Part B	Part C	Part D
Nativity				
General nativity	x		x	
Parental nativity	x	x	x	
Foreign White stock	x			
Specific nativity, by country of				
birth	x		x	
born in Puerto Rico			x	x
Occupations		x	x	x
Apportionment, Geography				
Selected states			x	
Selected Standard Metropolitan Areas		x		
Selected Indian areas		x	x	
New York City				x
Urban/rural	x	x	x	
Rural farm/nonfarm	x	x	x	

Decennial Year   1950

Census   Seventeenth Decennial Census

Volume   Volume IV Special Reports Part 4

Title   Mobility of the Population
         Part 4 A State of Birth
         Part 4 B Population Mobility - States and
               State Economic Areas
         Part 4 C Population Mobility - Farm and
               Nonfarm Movers
         Part 4 D Population Mobility - Characteris-
               tics of Migrants

Publication   Department of Commerce, Bureau of the Census
         Washington, DC: Government Printing Office

 Date   4 A 1953; 4 B 1956; 4 C and D 1957

Classifications

 Supt. of Documents C 3.950-7/6:pts.4 A, B, C and D

 Library of Congress HA 201.1950.A23 v.4 pts. 4 A, B, C, D

  card   52-60089 rev.

 Dewey   312.0973

 University of Texas 1950.130 through 1950.133

Microforms

 Research Pubns. Film 1950 Reel 17

Pages   4 A iv, 108; 4 B iv, 311; 4 C iv, 244; 4 D
         iv, 335 pages

Maps, illustrations None

Notes   This group of reports provides demographic
         and socioeconomic data on lifetime and recent
         mobility and migration.

1950
Volume IV Special Reports Parts 4 A, B, C and D

	Part A	Part B	Part C	Part D
Demographic Characteristics				
Aggregate population	x		x	x
Age	x	x	x	x
Race	x		x	x
Sex	x	x	x	x
Marital status		x	x	x
Social and Economic Characteristics				
Education	x	x		x
Employment/unemployment		x	x	x
Family		x		
Farmers, farms		x		
Households				x
Income		x	x	x
Labor force			x	x
Migration/mobility	x	x	x	x
State of birth	x	x	x	
State of residence	x			
In/out-migrants				x
Military/veterans				x
Nativity				
General nativity	x			
Specific nativity - native born by region of birth		x	x	
Occupations		x	x	x

1950
Volume IV Subject Reports Parts 4 A, B, C and D

	Part A	**Part B**	**Part C**	**Part D**
<u>Apportionment, Geography</u>				
Regions, divisions				x
State Economic Areas		x	x	
Economic Subregions			x	
Metropolitan/nonmetropolitan				x
Urban/rural				x
Rural farm/nonfarm				x

Decennial Year	1950
Census	Seventeenth Decennial Census
Volume	Volume IV Special Reports Part 5
Title	Other Subjects
	Part 5 A Characteristics by Size of Place
	Part 5 B Education
	Part 5 C Fertility
Publication	Department of Commerce, Bureau of the Census Washington, DC: Government Printing Office
Date	5 A and B 1953, 5 C 1955

Classifications

Supt. of Documents	C 3.950-7/6:pts.5 A, B and C
Library of Congress	HA 201.1950.A2 v.4 pts.5 A, B, C
card	52-60089 rev.
Dewey	312.0973
University of Texas	1950.134 through 1950.136

Microforms

Research Pubns.	Film 1950 Reel 17
Pages	5 A iv, 64; 5 B iv, 129; 5 C iv, 184 pages
Maps, illustrations	Maps and charts
Notes	Most tables based on 3 1/3 percent sample, some on 20 percent sample.

These reports were published as Series P-E, as preprints of Volume IV. They were never issued bound by the Census Bureau.

These reports include demographic and socio-economic data.

1950
Volume IV Special Reports Parts 5 A, B and C

	Part A	Part B	Part C
Demographic Characteristics			
Age	x	x	x
Race	x	x	x
Spanish surname - Whites only Limited to population of five southwestern states: Arizona, California, Colorado, New Mexico and Texas			x
Sex Limited to women aged 15-59 years	x	x	x x
Marital status By presence/absence of spouse	x	x	x x
Social and Economic Characteristics			
Education School enrollment Years of school completed	x	x x	x
Employment/unemployment	x	x	
Families	x		x
Farmers, farms	x		
Fertility			x
Income	x	x	
Labor force			x
Migration/mobility In District of Columbia	x	x	x x
Nativity Parental nativity	x	x x	x

1950
Volume IV   Special Reports   Parts 5 A, B and C

	Part A	Part B	Part C
Occupations	x	x	
Of husbands		x	
Apportionment, Geography			
Size of place	x		
Urban/rural		x	x
Farm/nonfarm		x	x
Vital Statistics			
Marriages			x
Duration			x

NOTES ON OTHER 1950 CENSUS PUBLICATIONS
WITH POPULATION INFORMATION

The four volumes of the 1950 Census include nearly all the data gleaned from the enumeration, both as to complete count and as to the sample questions. The final volumes, however, had been preceded by a number of separately printed reports. These include the following series:

P-A Series - <u>Number of Inhabitants</u> - Included as first chapters in Volumes I and II for each state.

P-B Series - <u>General Characteristics</u> - Included as second chapter in Volume II for each state.

P-C Series - <u>Detailed Characteristics</u> - Included as third chapter in Volume II for each state.

P-D Series - <u>Census Tract Statistics</u> - These reports actually became Volume III. Published in paper cover in 64 parts, each covering a tracted city or area, they were never reissued in bound form. The statistics in these reports superseded those published in the P-C-10 series below.

P-E Series - <u>Special Reports</u> - The 19 pieces in this series became Volume IV with its five parts, and like Volume III, it was never reissued in bound form.

Preliminary and Advance Reports

PC-1 Series - <u>Population of Selected Counties and Incorporated Places: April 1, 1950</u>

PC-2 Series - <u>Population of (State) by Counties: April 1, 1950</u>

PC-3 Series - <u>Population of (various areas)</u>

PC-4 Series - <u>Population of the Territories and Possessions: April 1, 1950</u>

PC-5 Series - <u>Characteristics of the Population of (specified Standard Metropolitan Area): April 1, 1950</u>

PC-6 Series - <u>Characteristics of the Population of (specified state, Hawaii and Puerto Rico): April 1, 1950</u>

PC-7 Series - <u>Characteristics of the Population (various subjects): April 1, 1950</u>

PC-8 Series - <u>Population of (specified) State: April 1, 1950</u>

PC-8A Series - <u>Population of (specified) State by Counties:</u>
<u>April 1, 1950</u>

PC-9 Series - <u>Population of the United States (various areas)</u>

PC-10 Series - <u>Population of (specified cities and adjacent areas)</u>
<u>by tracted areas: April 1, 1950</u>

PC-11 Series - <u>Population of Territories and Possessions</u>

PC-12 Series - <u>Characteristics of the Population of (specified)</u>
<u>State: April 1, 1950</u>

PC-14 Series - <u>Summary Reports of Population Characteristics</u>
<u>(various areas)</u>

Procedural Studies of the 1950 Census

Number 1 - Infant Enumeration Study

In an effort to determine the completeness of the enumeration,
an infant enumeration study was made in connection with the 1950
Census. Whenever an enumerator learned that a child had been born
during the first three months of 1950, s/he was to complete an "infant
card." Census records were then checked with birth records. A fol-
low-up letter was sent to parents when the child's name did not appear in the census records. The results of the comparison were published in this report.

   C 3.950-10:1   Research Pubns. Film 1950 Reel 18
                1953 vi, 64 pages

Number 2 - The 1950 Censuses - How They Were Taken

This is a lengthy explanation of the methodology used in taking and
compiling the reports from the 1950 Census.

   C 3.950-10:2   Research Pubns. Film 1950 Reel 18
                1955 vii, 222 pages

1950
Notes

Principal Data Collection Form Used in the 1950 Censuses

This publication contains facsimiles of the 18 enumeration forms
used in the 1950 Censuses of Population, Housing and Agriculture.
The major form for enumeration of the population and instructions to
enumerators can also be found at the end of Volume II Part I, which
is more readily available.

          C 33.950-2a:D262
          Research Pubns. Film 1950 Reel 18
          1952 41 pages

Alphabetic Index of Occupations and Industries: 1950

This publication, which listed occupations and industries for 1950,
prior to the enumeration, was intended for use in the classification
by code of those occupations and industries. It supersedes an edition
printed in 1948.

          C 3.950-2:Ocl
          Research Pubns. Film 1950 Reel 18
          1950 xxiv, 374 pages

Classified Index of Occupations and Industries

This publication also lists occupations and industries and desig-
nates the categories into which they are to be classified.

          C 3.950-2:Ocl/2
          Research Pubns. Film 1950 Reel 18
          1951 246 pages

Key to Published and Tabulated Data for Small Areas

This is a finding aid for statistics, for areas smaller than states,
available in published form or in unpublished form from the Census
Bureau, with directions for obtaining such data.

          C 3.2:D26/2
          Research Pubns. Film 1950 Reel 18
          1951 55 pages

1950
Notes

Farms and Farm People

Published in cooperation with the Department of Agriculture, this
was a special study combining information on population, housing, and
income data for the farm population.

> Research Pubns. Film 1950 Reel 19
> 1953   103 pages

1950 Monograph Series

The following publications were sponsored by the Bureau of the Census
and the Committee on Census Monographs of the Social Science Research Council. They were never published by the Census Bureau nor
by the Government Printing Office. Nor were any Superintendent of
Documents numbers ever assigned. They were published by Wiley & Sons
of New York City and by Chapman and Hall of London. They were written or otherwise prepared by a number of experts in the fields of the
subject matter. Accessed like any other privately published works
through normal library channels, they are listed here chronologically.

American Agriculture: Its Structure and Place in the Economy
   Ronald L. Mighell.   1955   197 pages   LC 55-8179

Income of the American People
   Herman P. Miller.   1955   220 pages   LC 55-9613

Immigrants and Their Children
   E.P. Hutchinson.   1956   402 pages   LC 56-6502

Social Characteristics of Urban and Rural Communities, 1950
   Otis Dudley Duncan and Albert J. Reiss, Jr.   1956   234 pages
   LC 56-7154

American Families
   Paul C. Glick.   1956   151 pages   LC 57-5910

American Housing and Its Use: The Demand for Shelter Space
   Louis Winnick and Ned Shilling.   1957   153 pages   LC 56-11034

Residential Finance
   Richard U. Ratcliff, Daniel B. Rathbun and Junia Honnold.   1957
   188 pages   LC 57-10813

Farm Housing
   Glenn J. Beyer and J. Hugh Rose.   1957   201 pages   LC 57-10802

1950
Notes

The Changing Population of the United States
   Conrad Taeuber and Irene B. Taeuber.   1957   316 pages   LC 57-13451

America's Children
   Eleanor J. Bernert.   1957   194 pages   LC 57-12298

The Older Population of the United States
   Harry D. Sheldon and Clark Tibbitts.   1958   233 pages   LC 58-6086

The Fertility of American Women
   Wilson H. Grabill, Clyde B. Kiser and Pascal K. Whelpton.   1958
   462 pages   LC 58-7899

The American Labor Force: Its Growth and Changing Composition
   Gertrude Bancroft.   1958   267 pages   LC 58-1079

The Educational Characteristics of the American People
   Sloan Wayland and Edmund deS. Brunner.   1958   262 pages   LC 58-59966
   (This publication, unlike the others, was distributed
   by Teachers College of Columbia University.)

STANDARD METROPOLITAN STATISTICAL AREAS OF THE UNITED STATES AND PUERTO RICO: 1960

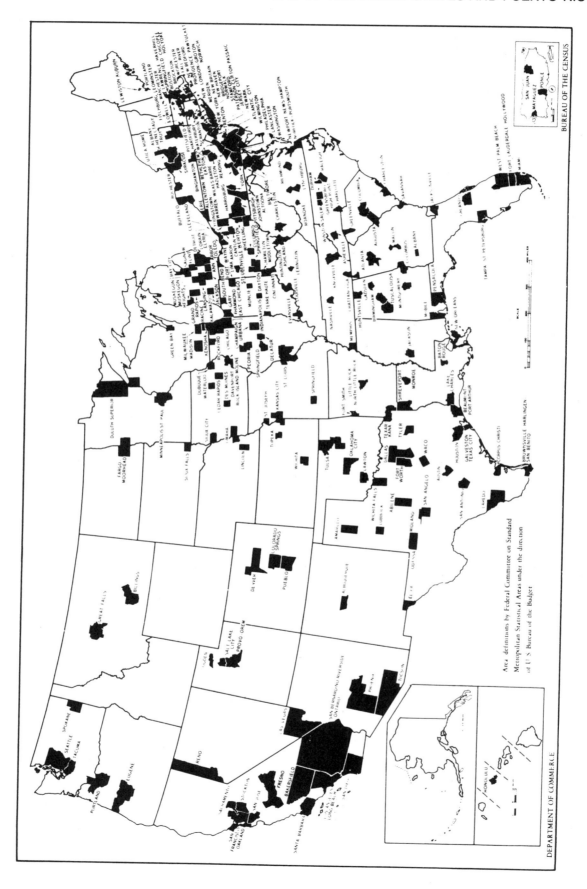

BUREAU OF THE CENSUS

Area definitions by Federal Committee on Standard Metropolitan Statistical Areas under the direction of U.S. Bureau of the Budget

DEPARTMENT OF COMMERCE

1960
POPULATION INFORMATION IN THE EIGHTEENTH DECENNIAL CENSUS

Major Population Reports

The volumes of the 1960 Census bear considerable resemblance to those of 1950. Bound in red, in contrast to the 1950 black, and numbered somewhat differently, Volume I is Characteristics of the Population, and Volume II is Subject Reports. Volume III includes the Selected Area Reports. There are a number of supplementary reports and a series of Census Tracts and six Census Monographs.

Volume I Part A, Number of Inhabitants provides the population counts for the entire United States, together with those for states and territories. Volume I Part 1 is the United States Summary and Parts 2 through 52 are separately bound parts for the states and the District of Columbia. Part 53 is Puerto Rico, and Parts 54-57 are a single book including data for all outlying territories. Each of these parts includes four chapters previously published as Series PC(1)A, PC(1)B, PC(1)C and PC(1)D. They include data on the number of inhabitants, general population characteristics, general social and economic characteristics, and detailed characteristics. The organization of the data is similar to that of the 1950 Census except for one additional chapter.

There are 56 separate Subject Reports which comprise Volume II. These reports were distributed separately in paper covers and were never provided in cloth binding by the Census Bureau. They make up eight groups covering race, ethnic data and language, mobility, families, children, education, employment, occupation, and one group of data on miscellaneous subjects.

The Selected Area Reports include those on size and type of place, on the Standard Metropolitan Statistical Areas, and on Americans abroad.

The six Census Monographs include ones on the Negro population, education, income distribution, rural population, mobility, and a longer analysis of the population, not completed until 1971. In addition, there were three monographs sponsored with the Social Science Research Council. These were not published by the Bureau and have no Superintendent of Documents classifications.

One hundred eighty separate Census Tract Reports were published, one for each Standard Metropolitan Statistical Area. Information in these reports includes the standard demographic characteristics as well as the information from the sample population questions and some data from the housing census.

1960
Introduction

Population Inquiries

Inquiries made to the entire population in 1960 were limited to sex, age, race, marital status and relationship to the head of the household. All other inquiries were on a sample basis. The latter characteristic was a change from the 1940 and 1950 Censuses, the 1940 Census being the first one where sampling was used. Another change was made in 1960: once the housing unit was designated as being in the sample, data for all members of that unit were taken and included in the sample.

Sample questions included those on education, farm residence, language, mobility, employment status, industry, occupation, place of and transportation to work, veteran status, marital history and for women, children ever borne. In 1960, place of birth of mother and father were returned to the enumerator's questionnaire. Like all censuses after 1940, a separate housing census was taken at the same time, with the results published in separate volumes under the title of Census of Housing.

States, Territories and Outlying Areas

The two remaining territories, those of Alaska and Hawaii, were admitted as states in 1959 and took their places in the alphabetical order of states in the census volumes for the first time. In Volume I a separate part was published for each state. Another part was published with data for the Commonwealth of Puerto Rico, and data for the possessions of American Samoa, the Canal Zone, Guam and the Virgin Islands appeared in a separate part entitled Outlying Areas.

1960
MAJOR POPULATION VOLUMES OF THE EIGHTEENTH DECENNIAL CENSUS

VOLUME	TITLE

Volume I   Characteristics of the Population

Part A   Number of Inhabitants
Part 1   United States Summary
Parts 2-57   States and Outlying Areas

Volume II   Subject Reports

1 A   Nativity and Parentage
1 B   Persons of Spanish Surname
1 C   Nonwhite Population by Race
1 D   Puerto Ricans in the United State
1 E   Mother Tongue of the Foreign Born

2 A   State of Residence and State of Birth
2 B   Mobility for States and State Economic Areas
2 C   Mobility for Metropolitan Areas
2 D   Lifetime and Recent Migration
2 E   Migration between State Economic Areas

3 A   Women by Number of Children Ever Born
3 B   Childspacing
3 C   Women by Children under Five Years Old

4 A   Families
4 B   Persons by Family Characteristics
4 C   Sources and Structure of Family Income
4 D   Age at First Marriage
4 E   Marital Status

5 A   School Enrollment
5 B   Educational Attainment
5 C   Socioeconomic Status

6 A   Employment Status and Work Experience
6 B   Journey to Work
6 C   Labor Reserve

1960
Major Population Volumes

VOLUME	TITLE	
Volume II (continued)	7 A	Occupational Characteristics
	7 B	Occupation by Earnings and Education
	7 C	Occupation by Industry
	7 D	Characteristics of Teachers
	7 E	Characteristics of Professional Workers
	7 F	Industrial Characteristics
	8 A	Inmates of Institutions
	8 B	Income of the Elderly Population
	8 C	Veterans
Volume III	Selected Area Reports	
	1 A	State Economic Areas
	1 B	Size of Place
	1 C	Americans Overseas
	1 D	Standard Metropolitan Statistical Areas
	1 E	Type of Place
Final Reports	Census Tracts	

Notes on other publications of the 1960 Census that contain population information are provided at the end of the 1960 section.

Decennial Year	1960
Census	Eighteenth Decennial Census
Volume	Volume I Part A
Title	Census of Population: 1960 Volume I Characteristics of the Population Part A Number of Inhabitants
Publication	Department of Commerce, Bureau of the Census Washington, DC: Government Printing Office
Date	1961

Classifications

Supt. of Documents	C 3.223/10:960/v.1/pt.A
Library of Congress	HA 201.1960.A2 v.1 pt.A
card	A 61-9570
Dewey	312.0973
University of Texas	1960.1

Microforms

Research Pubns.	Film 1960 Reel 1

Pages	xxxvi, 35 (maps and charts), 136 U.S. section; and separately numbered pages for each state and outlying area, totalling 1428 pages.
Maps, illustrations	Maps, charts, some in color at front of U.S. section. For each state, one map of counties, one of minor or census county divisions, and maps of urbanized areas.
Notes	This is a compilation of the Series PC(1)A reports for the U.S. as a whole, states and outlying areas with the final population count for each state, county, Standard Metropolitan Statistical Area, urbanized area, incorporated place, unincorporated places of 1,000, and minor civil divisions. The outlying areas are Puerto Rico, Guam, U.S. Virgin Islands, American Samoa and the Canal Zone.

1960
Volume I Characteristics of the Population Part A Number
of Inhabitants United States Summary Section

United States Summary Tables 1-41	United States	Regs., Divns.	States, O.Areas	Other
Demographic Characteristics				
Aggregate population	1	9	9	24
Historic from 1790	2	9-11	9-11	
Outlying areas				1
historic from 1940				1
Population abroad				1
historic from 1940				1
Rank of states			15,16	
historic from 1910			15	
Standard Metropolitan				
Statistical Areas	37			31,33, 35-37
Standard Consolidated Areas				32
Urbanized areas				22,23
Counties				24,26
historic from 1950				24
Cities				28,29
historic from 1790				28
Urban places				30
Congressional Districts			14	14
Economic Subregions				38
State Economic Areas			39	39
Areas with special censuses				
since 1950				40
Apportionment, Geography				
Apportionment	13		13	
Density	2,12	12	12	
Historic from 1790	2			
from 1910	12	12	12	
Urbanized areas, SMSA's				22,34

1960
Volume I Characteristics of the Population Part A Number
of Inhabitants United States Summary Section

United States Summary Tables 1-41	United States	Regs., Divns.	States, O.Areas	Other
Size of place (inhabitants)	5-8,21	21	21	
Historic from 1790	8			
SMSA's	18	18	18	
By type place	6			
Minor civil divisions - number				26,29
Incorporated places - number				27
Census tracts - number				41
Urban/rural	3,18,19	18,19	18,19	
Historic from earliest census	3,20	20	20	
Urban by 1940 special rules	4		4	4
Urbanized areas	17	17	17	

1960
Volume I   Characteristics of the Population   Part A   Number of Inhabitants   States and Outlying Areas Section

States and Outlying Areas* Tables 1-12	State	SMSAs	Counties	Places
Demographic Characteristics				
Aggregate population	1	12	7	5
Historic from earliest census	1			5
from 1940				8
Standard Metropolitan Statis- tical Areas		11,12		
Urbanized areas		10		10
historic from 1950		10		10
County minor civil divisions			7	7
Incorporated places				5,8
historic from 1940				8
of 10,000+ from earliest census				5
Unincorporated places of 1,000+				8
Areas annexed since 1950				9
Apportionment, Geography				
Density			6	
Size of place	2			
Historic from 1900	3			
Incorporated places, unincor- porated places, towns	4			
Urban/rural	1,4	12	6	
Historic from earliest census	1			

---

*Outlying areas have fewer tables.

Decennial Year	1960
Census	Eighteenth Decennial Census
Volume	Volume I Part 1
Title	Census of Population: 1960 Volume I Characteristics of the Population Part 1 United States Summary
Publication	Department of Commerce, Bureau of the Census Washington, DC: Government Printing Office
Date	1964

Classifications

Supt. of Documents	C 3.223/10:960/v.1/pt.1
Library of Congress	HA 201.1960.A2 v.1 pt.1
card	A 61-9570
Dewey	312.0973
University of Texas	1960.2

Microforms

Research Pubns.	Film 1960 Reel 2
Pages	cxxvii, S1-64, 823 pages
Maps, illustrations	119 pages of maps and charts on pages S1-64.
Notes	This volume, in addition to the introductory pages and the 64 illustrated pages at the beginning, includes four chapters originally published as PC(1) A, B, C and D.

1960
Volume I   Characteristics of the Population   Part 1   United States
Summary

	United States	Regions, Divisions, States, Counties	SMSAs, Urban Places
<u>Demographic Characteristics</u>			
Aggregate population	1,9,11	9,11,55	63,141, 151
Historic from 1790	2,9	9-11	
from 1910		15	
Puerto Rico, outlying areas		10,43,45, 48,55 60-62,67	
Counties		24	
historic from 1950		24	
Standard Metropolitan Statistical Areas			31
Standard Consolidated Areas			32
Urban places			28-30
Age	45	55,232-234	63,64
Single years of age	155-157		
By race	46,47,65	52,59	
by sex, historic from 1890	47		
by marital status	176		
Median age	60,287	60,287	
Cumulative age	159		
historic from 1900	160		
Persons 65+ years	55	55	
Race	42-44	51,56	63
White, Negro, Indian, Japanese, Chinese, Filipino, all other	44,56	56	
By age	46,155-160	233	
By sex	43-47, 57,65	51,57	
historic from 1860	44		
Sex	45-47		
By age	45,46		
By race	46,47		

1960
Volume I Characteristics of the Population Part 1 United States
Summary

	United States	Regions, Divisions, States, Counties	SMSAs, Urban Places
Marital status	48,49,60, 176-180	53,60,61	63,289
By age	176,179	252	
By race and sex	48		
By sex	61		
By presence of spouse	176,178		

Social and Economic Characteristics

Education			
School enrollment	73-75,114, 165-171, 273,274	102,104, 105,114, 239,240,	141,151, 153,306, 307,273, 274
historic from 1910	74		
public/private school	105,169	105	
Years of school completed	76,105, 172-174	102,104, 105,115,	141,151, 153,288, 308
historic from 1940	174		
Employment/unemployment	82,83, 119,194	103,104, 119,251, 253	142,143, 299
Historic from 1940	195		
Hours worked	194,197	253	
Weeks worked	85	254	300
Year last worked	200		
Class of employer	86		
Unemployed	90,194		
Families	78-80,124,	102,104	141,142
Married couples	79,80	118,243	141,153
Children under 18	281,282	281,282	290,291
By occupation of head	189		
By education of head	283	283	
Size of family	282	282	
Farmers, farms	86,124	124	

1960
Volume I   Characteristics of the Population   Part 1   United States Summary

	United States	Regions, Divisions, States, Counties	SMSAs, Urban Places
Fertility	55,81,105, 117,190- 193,284	55,102, 104,105, 117,284	63,141, 151,153, 294
Historic from 1910	81	284	
Households	50,55, 62,78, 117	54,55,62, 243,244	63
Group quarters	50,55, 62,182	54,55,62, 244,245, 280	63,290
Lodgers, resident employees	183		
Unrelated individuals	184,185		
Income			
Of families	95,96, 137-139, 224-231	103,104, 106,137- 139	142,148, 152,154, 301
Of persons	95-99,208, 215,217-223	103,104, 140	149,150
Industry	91,92, 124-125, 131-134, 209-215	103,104, 106,124, 125,131- 134,259-261	142,147, 154
Institutional population	50,82, 182,183	104,245	143,290
Labor force	82,84,120, 122,196, 285	104,106, 119,120, 122,252, 285	142,144, 152,154, 295
Historic from 1940	84		

1960
Volume I Characteristics of the Population Part 1 United States
Summary

	United States	Regions, Divisions, States, Counties	SMSAs, Urban Places
Language			
Mother tongue of the foreign born	70,111	105,111	141,151, 153
Migration/mobility	68,71,72, 100,109, 161	102,104, 105,112, 113,237, 238,272	141,151, 153,305
Military/veterans			
Veterans by period of service	77,116, 175,278	116,278	
Armed forces	82,83, 119,182, 194,195	104,119, 245,280	290
Nativity			
General and parental nativity	66,67,100, 105,108, 270	104,105, 108,270	141,151, 153
By age	155,156, 158-160	270	
By race	158		
Native born by age	235		
Foreign stock by country of origin	69,100, 110,162	104,110, 236	
Foreign born by country of origin	163		
Occupations	87-90,98, 126-130, 201-209	103,104, 126-130, 256-258	146
Historic from 1940	89		
Of unemployed	90		
Transportation to work	94,136, 216	104,106, 136	142,152, 154,303

196
Volume I Characteristics of the Population Part 1 United States Summary

	United States	Regions, Divisions, States, Counties	SMSAs, Urban Places
Apportionment, Geography			
Size of place	44,46,49, 50,100		
Urban/rural	42	58,108	
Age	46	52	
Race	42,43,46, 107	51-53,58, 107	
Sex	42,43,46	51-53,58	
Marital status	49	53	
Education	73,75,76		
Employment/unemployment	82,85,86,93		
Families	79,80		
Fertility	81		
Households	50,78	54	
Income	95-97,99	139	
Industry	91		
Labor force	82,84		
Language	70		
Migration/mobility	72		
Military/veterans	77		
Nativity	68,69		
Occupations	87,88,90		
Transportation	94		

Decennial Year	1960
Census	Eighteenth Decennial Census
Volume	Volume I Parts 2 through 57
Title	Census of Population: 1960 Volume I Characteristics of the Population Parts 2 through 57 States and Outlying Areas
Publication	Department of Commerce, Bureau of the Census Washington, DC: Government Printing Office
Date	1963
Supt of Documents	C 3.223/10:960/v.1/pts.2-57
Library of Congress	HA 201.1960.A2 v.1, pts. 2-57
Card	A 61-9570
Dewey	312.0973
University of Texas	1960.3 through 1960.55
Microforms	
Research Pubns	Film 1960 Reels 2 through 15
Pages	Pages vary
Maps, illustrations	Charts in introductory section, Part A: maps of counties, SMSAs, urbanized areas and large cities; Parts B and C: maps of counties and SMSAs. Brunsman, Chief, Population Division. Parts 2-52 are for States and the District of Columbia, Part 53 is for Puerto Rico, and Parts 54-57, in a single book, is for the outlying areas. This volume comprises Parts PC(1)-A, Parts PC(1)-B, Parts PC(1)-C and Parts PC(1)-D, the four series of bulletins for each state.

Volume I   Characteristics of the Population   Parts 2-57   States and Outlying Areas

	State	SMSA's	Counties	Places
Demographic Characteristics				
Aggregate population	1,12,35	11-13	6,7,13, 35,82	8
Historic from earliest census	1			
from 1940,1950			7	8
Minor civil divisions			7	
Incorporated places				5,8
historic				5,8
Areas annexed since 1950				9
Unincorporated places of 1,000				8
Urbanized areaas		10		8
Age	16,17,	20,71,	27	20,24, 26
Historic from 1890	17			
Single years	94			
Age groups, percent	13	13	13	13
By race and sex	16,37	20	27	20
by nativity	96,97	96	96	
By marital status	105	105	105	
Families, by age of head	109-112	109-112		
Of male veterans	104			
Race	14,15	21,72, 77,78	28-30, 87	21-23 72
White/nonwhite	14		27	
Individual races	14	21	28	21
By sex, historic from 1890	15			
Sex	14			
Historic from 1890	15			
By age and race	16	20	27	20
Marital status	13,108	13,21, 108	13,28-30 108	13,21- 23,25
Historic from 1940	18			
By race and sex	18			
Married couples	50		87	
By presence of spouse	105	105	105	
With/without own household	35,50	32	35	32

1960
Volume I   Characteristics of the Population   Parts 2-57   States
and Outlying Areas

	State	SMSA's	Counties	Places

Social and Economic Characteristics

	State	SMSA's	Counties	Places
Education				
School enrollment	35,44-46, 70,101	32,71 73,77	35,83 87	32,73 77
Private school enrollment	35,101	32	35	32
Years of school completed	35,47 70,102, 103	32,71 73,77, 103	35,83 87,91 93,103	32,34, 73,77, 81,102
Employment/unemployment	36,52, 53,70,71	33,71, 73,77	36,83, 87,91	33,34, 73,77
By age	115,117 123,128	115,117 123,128	93,115	81
By race and sex	53			
Hours worked	117	117		
by school enrollment	117	117		
Weeks worked in 1959	36,55, 118	33,76, 118	36,86, 118	33,76
Year last worked	119	119	119	
By class of employer	56	74	84	74
Place of work	36,63	33,72,77	36,87	33,72, 77
Unemployed persons	53	75,78	83,88	34,75, 78
Families	35,50,70, 108-112	32,108- 112	35,82, 108	32
By age of head	109,110	109,110		
By race	50,110	110	87	
By size	110	110		
Children	35,50, 109,110, 114	32	35,82	32
Living with both parents	70		87	
By education of head	111	111		
By number in labor force	111	111		
By occupation of head	112	112		
Farmers, farms	56		35,91-93	
Fertility	51,113	72,77	82,87, 113,114	72,77

1960
Volume I Characteristics of the Population Parts 2-57 States and Outlying Areas

	State	SMSA's	Counties	Places
Households	13,19, 49,71,106	13,21 71,106	13,28-31 92	13,21, 31
Number, persons per household	13,49	13	13	13
Group quarters	13,49,107	13,21,107	13,28,92	
Income	65-67,133	76,78,133	86,88,93	76,78
Historic from 1950	66,67			
Of families	36,65, 139-146	33,78 139-146	36,86, 88,91,93	33,34, 78,81
Of persons	67,133- 138	76,78, 133-138	86,88, 134	76,78, 134
Earnings	69,124 130,132	76,124, 130	86	76
by occupation	68		86	
Industry	61,125- 127,129	75,78, 125,127, 129	85,88 127	75,78, 81
Institutional population	52,107	21,107	28,87,92	21
Labor force	33,36,52, 70,71, 116	33,71, 73,93, 116	36,83, 87,93	33,34, 73
By sex, marital status	36,52	33	36	33
Women, children -6 years	36,70		36	
Males 65+ years	36		36	
Language				
Mother tongue of foreign born	41	32,80	90	32,80
Migration/mobility	35,42, 43,70	72,77	35,82	72,77
Residing in state of birth	35,39	32	35	32
Moved after 1958	35	32	35	32
Residence in 1955	42,100	77	82	72,77
Military/veterans	48,104	72		72
Armed forces	53		83	

1960
Volume I Characteristics of the Population Parts 2-57 States and Outlying Areas

	State	SMSA's	Counties	Places
Nativity				
General nativity	35,38, 70,71	32,71 72	35,82 91,93	32,34, 72,81
Native of foreign or mixed parentage	35	32,72	35,82, 91,93	32,34 72,81
Specific nativity				
native by region	98			98
foreign born by country	99	99		
foreign stock by country	40,70,71	71,79,99	89	79
Occupations	36,57,58, 120-122	33,74,78, 121-122	36,84, 88,91, 121	33,74, 78,81
Historic from 1940	59			
from 1950	120			
Of the unemployed	60			
Transportation to work	64	33,72	36,82	33,72

Apportionment, Geography

	State	SMSA's	Counties	Places
Density	6		6	
Size of place	2-4,14, 70			
Historic from 1900	3			
Urban/rural	1,13,14, 16,70,71	13	13,91,92	13
Historic from earliest census	1			
Age	16,37			
Race, by sex	14,16,17, 37			
Marital status	18,50,105	105	105	
Education	44,46,47			
Employment	52,55,117	117		
Families	50,108- 110	108-110	108	
Households	49,71			
Income	65-67,69 133,134	133,134	134	
Industry	61			

1960
Volume I Characteristics of the Population Parts 2-57 States and Outlying Areas

	State	SMSA's	Counties	Places
Urban/rural (continued)				
Institutional population				
Labor force	52,70,71			
Language	41			
Migration/mobility	42,43			
Military/veterans	48			
Nativity	38-40,71			
Occupations	57,58			
Transportation	64			

Decennial Year   1960

Census   Eighteenth Decennnial Census

Volume   Volume II   Subject Reports   Part 1

Titles   1 A   Nativity and Parentage
                            1 B   Persons of Spanish Surname
                            1 C   Nonwhite Population by Race
                            1 D   Puerto Ricans in the United States
                            1 E   Mother Tongue of the Foreign Born

Publication   Department of Commerce, Bureau of the Census
                            Washington, DC: Government Printing Office

  Date   1 A 1965; 1 B, C, D 1963; 1 E 1966

Classifications

  Supt. of Documents   C 3.223/10:960/v.2/pts.1 A, B, C, D, E

  Library of Congress   HA 201.1960.A2 v.2 pts.1 A, B, C, D, E

    card   A 61-9570

  Dewey   312.0973

  University of Texas   1960.56 through 1960.60

Microforms

  Research Pubns.   Film 1960   Reels 15,16

Pages   1 A xiv, 153;   1 B xvii, 202;   1 C xix, 255;
                            1 D xiv, 104;   1 E xiii, 25 pages

Maps, illustrations   Part 1 A Maps of Census Regions and Geo-
                            graphic Divisions.

Notes   Part A provides data on foreign born and
                            persons of foreign stock. Part B is limited
                            to the White population of the 5 southwestern
                            states: Arizona, California, Colorado, New
                            Mexico and Texas. In Part C, the races iden-
                            tified are Negro, Indian, Japanese, Chinese,
                            Filipino and all others. Part D is limited
                            to persons of Puerto Rican birth or parentage.
                            Part E provides information on the mother
                            tongue of the foreign born.

1960
Volume II   Subject Reports   Parts 1 A, B, C, D and E

	A	B	Part C	D	E
<u>Demographic Characteristics</u>					
Aggregate Population	x				
Coterminous U.S. 1900-1960	x				
Persons of Puerto Rican birth				x	
Age	x	x	x	x	x
Race	x		x	x	x
Limited to Whites of Spanish surname		x			
Negro, Indian, Japanese, Chinese and Filipino, all others			x		
Spanish surname					
Limited to White population of Spanish surname in 5 SW states		x			x
Sex	x	x	x	x	x
Marital status	x	x	x	x	
<u>Social and Economic Characteristics</u>					
Education					
School enrollment		x	x	x	
Years of school completed	x	x	x	x	x
Employment/unemployment		x	x	x	
Hours worked		x	x	x	
Weeks worked		x	x	x	
Families		x	x	x	
By size		x	x	x	
Primary/secondary families		x	x	x	
Employment of family members		x		x	
Households		x	x	x	
Group quarters		x	x	x	
Income		x	x	x	

1960
Volume II Subject Reports Parts 1 A, B, C, D and E

	A	B	Part C	D	E
Industry		x	x	x	
Institutional population		x	x	x	
Labor force		x	x	x	
Language		x			x
Mother tongue of foreign born,					x
Mother tongue of White popula-					
tion coterminous states					x
historic from 1930					x
Migration/mobility		x	x	x	
Military/veterans		x	x		
Nativity					
General nativity	x	x	x		
Foreign born by country of					
origin		x			x
Mexico			x		
Puerto Rico				x	
Canada	x				
Parentage	x	x		x	
Occupations	x	x	x	x	

Apportionment, Geography

	A	B	C	D	E
Regions					x
States	x			x	x
5 SW states		x			
Alaska, Hawaii			x		
Metropolitan Statistical Areas	x	x		x	x
Counties		x			x
Urban areas					x
Urban/rural		x	x	x	
Rural farm/nonfarm		x	x	x	

Decennial Year	1960
Census	Eighteenth Decennial Census
Volume	Volume II Subject Reports Part 2
Titles	2 A State of Residence and State of Birth
	2 B Mobility for States and State Economic Areas
	2 C Mobility for Metropolitan Areas
	2 D Lifetime and Recent Migration
	2 E Migration between State Economic Areas
Publication	Department of Commerce, Bureau of the Census Washington, DC: Government Printing Office
Date	2 A, B, C and D 1963; 2 E 1967
Classifications	
Supt. of Documents	C 3.223/10:960/v.2/pts.2 A, B, C, D, E
Library of Congress	HA 201.1960.A2 v.2 pts.2 A, B, C, D, E
card	A 61-9570
Dewey	312.0973
University of Texas	1960.61 through 1960.64
Microforms	
Research Pubns.	Film 1960 Reels 16 and 17
Pages	2 A xiii, 177; 2 B xxii, 468; 2 C xvii, 348; 2 D xiii, 493; 2 E xvi, 372 pages
Maps, illustrations	Parts A, B and C, maps of Census Regions and Geographic Divisions; Parts B-E, also map of Economic Subregions and State Economic Areas; Part C, Standard Metropolitan Statistical Areas.
Notes	Parts A and D relate recent and lifetime migration and demographic area social characteristics. Parts B and C provide mobility data for states, State Economic Areas and Standard Metropolitan Areas. Part E is limited to State Economic Area migration.

1960
Volume II   Subject Reports   Parts 2 A, B, C, D and E

	A	B	Part C	D	E
Demographic Characteristics					
Aggregate population	x				
Limited to population 5+ years		x	x	x	x
Historic from 1850	x				
Age	x		x	x	
Limited to persons 5+ years		x	x	x	
Race					
White/nonwhite	x	x	x	x	
Sex	x	x	x	x	
Marital status		x			
Social and Economic Characteristics					
Education					
School enrollment		x			
Years of school completed		x	x	x	
College students		x			
by area of residence		x			
Employment/unemployment		x	x		
Family		x	x		
Households		x	x		
Group quarters		x			
Housing		x			
Tenure		x			
Income		x	x		
Institutional population		x	x		

1960
Volume II   Subject Reports   Parts 2 A, B, C, D and E

	A	B	Part C	D	E
Migration/mobility	x	x	x	x	x
Historic from 1950	x				
Residence in 1955		x	x	x	x
Persons 16-34 in college not living with parents		x			
Net migration	x				
Military		x			
Armed forces		x			
Veterans by period of service		x			
Nativity					
General nativity	x				
State, region of birth	x				
Born in outlying areas	x				
Born abroad or at sea	x				
Occupations		x	x		

Apportionment, Geography

	A	B	Part C	D	E
Regions	x	x		x	
Divisions	x	x		x	
States	x	x	x	x	
Urban/rural		x			
Rural farm/nonfarm		x			
State Economic Areas and Subregions			x		
Standard Metropolitan Areas	x		x		
Metropolitan/nonmetropolitan			x		

Decennial Year	1960
Census	Eighteenth Decennial Census
Volume	Volume II Subject Reports Part 3
Titles	3 A Women by Number of Children Ever Born
	3 B Childspacing
	3 C Women by Children under Five Years Old
Publication	Department of Commerce, Bureau of the Census Washington, DC: Government Printing Office
Date	3 A 1964; 3 B and C 1968

Classifications

Supt. of Documents	C 3.223/10:960/v.2/pts.3 A, B, C
Library of Congress	HA 201.1960.A2 v.2 pts. 3 A, B, C
card	A 61-9570
Dewey	312.0973
University of Texas	3 A and B 1960.65 and 1960.66; 3 C 1960.66-1

Microforms

Research Pubns.	Film 1960 Reel 17
Pages	3 A xx, 323; 3 B xxi, 185; 3 C xx, 140 pages
Maps, illustrations	Each part has a map of Census Regions and Geographic Divisions.
Notes	All three parts provide data on demographic, social and economic characteristics. Part A provides information on fertility. Part B provides data on births to women of child-bearing age and intervals between births. Part C has data on children under five and also on children aged five to nine.

1960
Volume II Subject Reports Parts 3 A, B and C

	Part A	Part B	Part C
Demographic Characteristics			
Aggregate population			
Limited to women 15+ years	x		x
Most tables limited to women 14-39 years		x	
Age	x	x	x
Of wife, of husband	x		x
Of children - under 5, 5-9 years			x
Race	x	x	x
Spanish surname			
Five southwestern states	x		x
Puerto Rico	x		x
Sex	x	x	x
Marital status	x	x	x
Social and Economic Characteristics			
Education			
Years of school completed	x	x	x
wife	x	x	x
husband	x		x
Families	x	x	x
Farmers, farms	x	x	
Fertility	x	x	x
Households	x		x
Group quarters			x
Housing	x		x
Income			
Family	x		x
Husband	x	x	x
Institutional population	x		x

1960
Volume II Subject Reports Parts 3 A, B and C

	Part A	Part B	Part C
Labor force	x	x	x
Migration/mobility	x		x
Nativity			
General nativity	x		x
Natives by region of birth	x		x
Foreign born, stock by country of origin	x		x
Parentage	x		x
Occupations			
Wife	x	x	x
Husband	x	x	x
Apportionment, Geography			
Size of place	x		
Urban/rural	x	x	x
Rural farm/nonfarm	x	x	x
Regions	x	x	x
The South	x	x	x
Metropolitan/nonmetropolitan	x		x
Urbanized areas	x	x	x
Vital Statistics			
Births	x	x	x
Rate	x	x	
Marriages	x	x	x
Times married, duration	x	x	x
Year of, years since first married	x	x	x
Age at first marriage	x	x	x

Decennial Year	1960
Census	Eighteenth Decennial Census
Volume	Volume II Subject Reports Part 4
Titles	4 A Families 4 B Persons by Family Characteristics 4 C Sources and Structure of Family Income 4 D Age at First Marriage 4 E Marital Status
Publication	Department of Commerce, Bureau of the Census Washington, DC: Government Printing Office
Date	4 A 1963; 4 B and C 1964; 4 D and E 1966
Classifications	
Supt. of Documents	C 3.223/10:960/v.2/pts.4 A, B, C, D, E
Library of Congress	HA 201.1960.A2 v.2 pts.4 A, B, C, D, E
card	A 61-9570
Dewey	312.0973
University of Texas	1960.67 through 1960.71
Microforms	
Research Pubns.	Film 1960 Reels 17 and 18
Pages	4 A xxiv, 453; 4 B xxii, 205; 4 C xx, 235; 4 D xxii, 172; 4 E xviii, 173 pages
Maps, illustrations	Parts A, C and D each have maps of Census Regions and Geographic Divisions.
Notes	The titles of these reports clearly present a description of their contents. Demographic, social and economic characteristics are pro- vided for each of the five parts.

1960
Volume II   Subject Reports   Parts 4 A, B, C, D and E

	A	B	Part C	D	E
<u>Demographic Characteristics</u>					
Age	x	x	x	x	x
Race	x	x	x	x	x
Spanish heritage				x	
Sex	x	x	x	x	x
Marital status	x	x	x	x	x
<u>Social and Economic Characteristics</u>					
Education	x	x	x	x	x
Employment/unemployment	x		x	x	
Families	x	x	x		
Farmers/farms	x	x	x		x
Households	x	x	x	x	
Housing	x	x	x	x	
Income	x	x	x	x	x
Industry		x			
Institutional population		x			
Labor force	x				
Migration/mobility	x	x			
Nativity	x			x	x
Occupations	x	x		x	x
Transportation		x			

1960
Volume II   Subject Reports   Parts 4 A, B, C, D and E

	A	B	Part C	D	E
Apportionment, Geography					
Urban/rural	x	x	x	x	x
Rural farm/nonfarm	x	x	x	x	
Urbanized areas		x	x		x
Regions			x		x
The South		x	x		x
New York City				x	
Vital Statistics					
Marriages				x	x
Age at first marriage				x	
Duration of marriages				x	
Times married				x	x

Decennial Year	1960
Census	Eighteenth Decennial Census
Volume	Volume II Subject Reports Part 5
Titles	5 A School Enrollment 5 B Educational Attainment 5 C Socioeconomic Status
Publication	Department of Commerce, Bureau of the Census Washington, DC: Government Printing Office
Date	5 A 1964; 5 B 1963; 5 C 1967
Classifications	
Supt. of Documents	C 3.223/10:960/v.2/pts.5 A, B, C
Library of Congress	HA 201.1960.A2 v.2 pts. 5 A, B, C
card	A 61-9570
Dewey	312.0973
University of Texas	1960.72 through 1960.74
Microforms	
Research Pubns.	Film 1960 Reel 18
Pages	5 A xviiii, 132; 5 B xvi, 188; 5 C xix, 268 p¯ges
Maps, illustrations	Parts 5 B and 5 C, maps of Census Regions and Geographic Divisions.
Notes	Each of the three parts includes most demo- graphic as well as social and economic char- acteristics as variables.

74

1960
Volume II   Subject Reports   Parts 5 A, B and C

	Part A	**Part B**	**Part C**
Demographic Characteristics			
Aggregate population		x	x
Age	x	x	x
Limited to persons 5 through 34 years	x		
Race	x	x	x
Sex	x	x	x
Marital status	x	x	x
Absence/presence of spouse	x		
Social and Economic Characteristics			
Education			
School enrollment	x		
College enrollment	x		
Years of school completed		x	
Education of parents	x		
Persons not enrolled in school/college	x		
Employment	x	x	
Of parent	x		
Families	x	x	x
Persons enrolled and living with parents	x		
Presence of own children		x	
By stage of family life cycle			x
Fertility			x
Households	x		x
Living arrangements of college students	x		
Housing			
Tenure			x
Income	x	x	x
Contribution to family by those not enrolled in school	x		
Contribution of wife			x

1960
Volume II   Subject Reports   Parts 5 A, B and C

	Part A	Part B	Part C
Labor force	x	x	
Military/veterans			
Armed forces	x	x	
Nativity	x	x	x
General nativity	x		
Native born – region of birth	x	x	
Foreign stock – region	x	x	x
Foreign born – region of birth	x	x	
Parental nativity	x	x	
Occupations	x	x	x

Apportionment, Geography

	Part A	Part B	Part C
Size of place	x	x	
Regions		x	x
Urbanized areas	x	x	x
Urban/rural		x	x
Rural farm/nonfarm	x	x	x
Metropolitan/nonmetropolitan areas			x

Decennial Year	1960
Census	Eighteenth Decennial Census
Volume	Volume II Subject Reports Part 6
Titles	6 A Employment Status and Work Experience 6 B Journey to Work 6 C Labor Reserve
Publication	Department of Commerce, Bureau of the Census Washington, DC: Government Printing Office
Date	6 A and B 1963; 6 C 1966
Classifications	
Supt. of Documents	C 3.223/10:960/v.2/pts.6 A, B, C
Library of Congress	HA 201.1960.A2 v.2 pts. 6 A, B, C
card	A 61-9570
Dewey	312.0973
University of Texas	1960.75 through 1960.77
Microforms	
Research Pubns.	Film 1960 Reel 19
Pages	6 A xxii, 226; 6 B xv, 564; 6 C xix, 199 pages
Maps, illustrations	Part B has map of Standard Metropolitan Statistical Areas.
Notes	Part A provides demographic, social and economic characteristics in relation to employment. Part B relates place of residence, of work, and means of transportation to named metropolitan areas. Part C is confined to demographic, social and economic characteristics of persons in the labor reserve.

1960
Volume II Subject Reports Parts 6 A, B and C

	Part A	Part B	Part C
<u>Demographic Characteristics</u>			
Aggregate population			
Limited to persons 14+ years	x		
Limited to persons in labor force since 1950, who were neither "employed" nor "unemployed" in 1960			x
Age	x	x	x
Race	x	x	x
Sex	x	x	x
Marital status	x		x
<u>Social and Economic Characteristics</u>			
Education			
School enrollment	x		x
Years of school completed	x		x
Employment	x		x
Class of employer			x
Year last worked			x
Place of work		x	
Weeks, hours worked 1959	x		x
Family	x	x	
Farmers, farms	x		x
Fertility	x		x
Households	x	x	x
Group quarters			x
Income	x	x	x
Of women other than earnings			x
Industry		x	x
Institutional population			x

1960
Volume II Subject Reports Parts 6 A, B and C

	Part A	Part B	Part C
Labor force			
Labor reserve			x
income other than earnings			x
women by age and number of children			x
women 50+ years			x
Migration/mobility			x
Occupations			x
Transportation to work			
Limited to workers and/or residents of Standard Metropolitan Statistical Areas of 250,000+ population		x	
Apportionment, Geography			
Urban/rural	x	x	
Farm/nonfarm	x	x	
Standard Metropolitan Statistical Areas		x	
Components, contiguous counties		x	
Urbanized areas, central cities		x	

Decennial Year	1960
Census	Eighteenth Decennial Census
Volume	Volume II Subject Reports Part 7
Titles	7 A Occupational Characteristics 7 B Occupations by Earnings and Education 7 C Occupation by Industry 7 D Characteristics of Teachers 7 E Characteristics of Professional Workers 7 F Industrial Characteristics
Publication	Department of Commerce, Bureau of the Census Washington, DC: Government Printing Office
Date	7 A, B and C 1963; 7 D and E 1964; 7 F 1967
Classifications	
Supt. of Documents	C 3.223/10:960/v.2/pts.7 A, B, C, D, E, F
Library of Congress	HA 201.1960.A2 v.2 pts. 7 A, B, C, D, E, F
card	A 61-9570
Dewey	312.0973
University of Texas	1960.78 through 1960.82 (Part 7 F not listed)
Microforms	
Research Pubns.	Film 1960 Reels 19 and 20
Pages	7 A xxi, 530; 7 B xiv, 304; 7 C xvii, 146; 7 D xvi, 58; 7 E xvi, 145; 7 F xx, 195
Maps, illustrations	Parts 7 B, D, E and F each have a map of Census Regions and Geographic Divisions.
Notes	This group of reports relates occupations and industries to demographic, social and eco- nomic characteristics of those employed in each. Separate reports are included on all professional groups and on teachers in primary, secondary and higher education.

1960
Volume II   Subject Reports   Parts 7 A, B, C, D, E and F

	A	B	Part C	D	E	F
Demographic Characteristics						
Aggregate population						
Limited to persons 14+ years	x		x	x		x
Limited to men 18-64 years		x				
Limited to employed labor force					x	
Age	x	x	x	x	x	x
Race	x	x		x	x	x
Sex	x		x	x		x
Limited to men		x				
Marital status	x			x	x	x
Social and Economic Characteristics						
Education						
Years of school completed	x	x		x	x	
Employment	x		x		x	x
Hours worked					x	x
Weeks worked 1959	x			x	x	
Year last worked	x			x	x	
Class employer	x		x		x	x
Unpaid family member	x					
Self-employed						x
Family	x			x		x
Household						x
Housing	x					
Income	x	x		x	x	x
Industry	x		x			x
Labor force	x	x		x	x	
Labor reserve	x			x		

1960
Volume II   Subject Reports   Parts 7 A, B, C, D, E and F

	A	B	Part C	D	E	F
Nativity						
Native born by region of birth	x					
Occupations	x	x	x	x	x	
Of spouse				x		
<u>Apportionment, Geography</u>						
Urban/rural	x			x	x	x
Farm/nonfarm				x	x	
Urbanized areas				x	x	
Regions		x		x	x	
The South		x				

Decennial Year	1960
Census	Eighteenth Decennial Census
Volume	Volume II Subject Reports Part 8
Titles	8 A Inmates of Institutions 8 B Income of the Elderly Population 8 C Veterans
Publication	Department of Commerce, Bureau of the Census Washington, DC: Government Printing Office
Date	8 A and B 1963; 8 C 1964

Classifications

Supt. of Documents	C 3.223/10:960/v.2/pts.8 A, B, C
Library of Congress	HA 201.1960.A2 v.2 pts. 8 A, B, C
card	A 61-9570
Dewey	312.0973
University of Texas	1960.83 through 1960.85

Microforms

Research Pubns.	Film 1960 Reels 20 and 21
Pages	8 A xix, 303; 8 B xii, 207; 8 C xv, 99 pages
Maps, illustrations	Part A, one map of Standard Metropolitan Statistical Areas.
Notes	The first of these reports includes demographic information as well as education and nativity data on inmates and considerable information on named institutions. Information on the elderly is limited by demographic, family and income data. The third report is limited to male veterans. Subject reports were issued in blue paper covers, not bound.

1960
Volume II Subject Reports Parts 8 A, B and C

	Part A	Part B	Part C
Demographic Characteristics			
Aggregate population	x		x
Age	x		x
Limited to persons 65+ years and their families		x	
Limited to persons 18+ years			x
Race	x		x
Sex	x	x	
Limited to males			x
Marital status	x		x
Times married			x
Social and Economic Status			
Education			
School enrollment	x		
Years of school completed			x
Employment/unemployment			x
Weeks worked 1959			x
Families		x	x
Number children			x
Veteran head of family			x
Households			x
Housing			
Tenure			x
value of owner-occupied homes			x
Income			
Family and unrelated individuals		x	x
Husband/wife income		x	
Source of income			x

1960
Volume II Subject Reports Parts 8 A, B and C

	Part A	Part B	Part C
Institutional population	x		
By type of institution	x		
mental hospitals	x		
residential treatment centers	x		
tuberculosis hospitals	x		
chronic disease hospitals	x		
homes, schools for mentally handicapped	x		
homes, schools for physically handi-capped	x		
homes, schools for dependent and neglected children	x		
training schools for juvenile delinquents, diagnostic centers	x		
By year of admission	x		
By type of control	x		
By size of institution	x		
Labor force			x
Migration/mobility	x		
Migration after 1955			x
Region of residence/region of birth	x		
Military			x
By period of service			x
Nativity	x		
Occupations			x

Apportionment, Geography

	Part A	Part B	Part C
Urban/rural			x
Urban/rural nonfarm	x		x
Inside/outside metropolitan areas	x	x	

Decennial Year   1960

Census   Eighteenth Decennial Census

Volume   Volume III   Selected Area Reports

Titles   1 A   State Economic Areas
                          1 B   Size of Place
                          1 C   Americans Overseas
                          1 D   Standard Metropolitan Statistical Areas
                          1 E   Type of Place

Publication   Department of Commerce, Bureau of the Census
                          Washington, DC: Government Printing Office

Date   1 A and D 1963; 1 B, C and E 1964

Classifications

Supt. of Documents   C 3.223/10:960/v.3/pts.1 A, B, C, D, E

Library of Congress   HA 201.1960.A2 v.3 pts.1 A, B, C, D, E

   card   A 61-9570

Dewey   312.0973

University of Texas   1960.86 through 1960.90

Microforms

Research Pubns.   Film 1960   Reel 21

Pages   1 A xviii, 464; 1 B xix, 78; 1 C xix, 132;
                          1 D xx, 747; 1 E xviii, 459 pages

Maps, illustrations   Part A, maps of 509 State Economic Areas;
                          Parts B and E, Census Regions and Geographic
                          Divisions; Parts D and E, Standard Metropoli-
                          tan Statistical Areas.

Notes   Part A has demographic, social and economic
                          data on named state economic areas. Part B
                          has data on urbanized areas and urban places.
                          Part C has data results from a special ques-
                          tionnaire sent to Americans abroad. It includ-
                          ed the only question on citizenship in 1960.
                          Part D has data on named SMSAs. Part E has
                          data by type of place.

1960
Volume III   Selected Area Reports   Parts 1 A, B, C, D and E

	A	B	Part C	D	E
Demographic Characteristics					
Aggregate population	x	x		x	x
Persons abroad			x		
by year left the U.S.			x		
Age	x	x	x	x	x
Race	x	x		x	x
Sex	x	x	x	x	x
Marital status	x	x	x	x	x
By presence/absence of spouse				x	
Social and Economic Characteristics					
Citizenship			x		
Education					
School enrollment	x	x	x		
Years of school completed	x	x	x	x	x
Degrees			x		
Field of study			x		
Employment/unemployment	x	x	x	x	x
Place of work inside/outside					
county of residence	x	x			
By class of employer			x		
Federal employees			x		
by occupation			x		
Families	x		x	x	x
Married couples	x	x			x
with/without own households	x	x			
with own children	x	x		x	
Fertility					
Children ever born	x	x		x	x
by marital status of parent				x	
by age of mother				x	

1960
Volume III   Selected Area Reports   Parts 1 A, B, C, D and E

	A	B	Part C	D	E
Households	x	x	x		x
Group quarters	x	x			x
Income	x			x	x
Industry	x		x	x	x
Labor force	x	x		x	
Married women				x	
Language					
Ability to speak local language			x		
Migration/mobility	x		x		
State of birth	x				
Residence in 1955	x	x		x	
Year moved into present house	x	x	x		
Military					
Armed forces	x	x	x		
dependent			x		
Nativity					
General nativity	x	x		x	x
Specific – by country of birth	x	x			
by area of birth			x		
Parental nativity			x	x	x
Occupations	x	x	x	x	x
Transportation to work	x	x			

Apportionment, Geography

	A	B	Part C	D	E
Regions		x			
The South		x			
State Economic Subregions and State Economic Areas	x				
Standard Metropolitan Statistical Areas				x	x

1960
Volume III   Selected Area Reports   Parts 1 A, B, C, D and E

	A	B	Part C	D	E
Urbanized areas		x			x
Urban/rural	x				x
Rural farm/nonfarm	x				x
Size of place		x		x	
Central cities/urban fringe				x	

Decennial Year	1960
Census	Eighteenth Decennial Census
Volume	Final Reports
Title	Census Tracts
Publication	Department of Commerce, Bureau of the Census Washington, DC: Government Printing Office
Date	1961-1962

Classifications

Supt. of Documents	C 3.223/10:960/1-180
Library of Congress	HA 201.1960.A2 v.3 pts.1-180
card	A 61-9570
Dewey	312.0973
University of Texas	1960.92 through 1960.272

Microforms

Research Pubns.	Film 1960 Reels 22-30
Pages	Vary from 26 to 1,060 pages
Maps, illustrations	There is a separate sheet map of census tracts enclosed with each part.
Notes	A separate unbound publication was published for each of the 180 Standard Metropolitan Statistical Areas following the 1960 Census. The reports included data from both the Population and the Housing Censuses. For areas with considerable Negro or Spanish-surnamed population, additional tables were provided with data on that population.

Final reports Series PHC(1) |

1960
Final Reports   Census Tracts

	SMSA	Component Parts	Tracts
Demographic Characteristics			
Aggregate population	P1	P1	P1
Age	P2,5	P2,5	P2,5
Race	P1,2	P1,2	P1,2
Nonwhite	P4	P4	P4
Spanish surname – White only	P1,5	P1,5	P1,5
Puerto Rican birth or parentage	P5	P5	P5
Sex	P2,5	P2,5	P2,5
Marital status	P2,5	P2,5	P2,5
Social and Economic Characteristics			
Education			
School enrollment	P1,4	P1,4	P1,4
Years of school completed	P1,5	P1,5	P1,5
Employment/unemployment	P3,4,5	P3,4,5	P3,4,5
Class of employer	P3	P3	P3
Place of work	P3	P3	P3
Families	P1,4	P1,4	P1,4
Households	P1,4	P1,4	P1,4
Group quarters	P1	P1	P1
Housing	H1-3	H1-3	H1-3
Income	P1,4,5	P1,4,5	P1,4,5
Industry	P3	P3	P3
Institutional population	P1	P1	P1
Labor force	P3,4,5	P3,4,5	P3,4,5
Migration/mobility	P1,4,H2	P1,4,H2	P1,4,H2

1960
Final Reports Census Tracts

	SMSA	Component Parts	Tracts
Nativity			
General nativity	P1	P1	P1
Parentage	P1	P1	P1
Foreign stock	P1	P1	P1
Occupations	P3,4	P3,4	P3,4
Transportation	P3,H2	P3,H2	P3,H2

NOTES ON OTHER 1960 CENSUS PUBLICATIONS
WITH POPULATION INFORMATION

VOLUME	TITLE

Supplementary Reports

There were 56 Supplementary Reports published as the result of the 1960 enumeration. The data in those reports were final data, and some were published prior to the major volumes in which they also appeared. Most of the reports were quite short, less than a dozen pages. The series was numbered PC(S)1 by the Census Bureau.

C 3.223/12:960/1 through 56

1. Population of Standard Metropolitan Statistical Areas: 1950 and 1960. 19 pages. 1961.

2. Population of Congressional Districts: April 1, 1960. 7 pages. 1961.

3. Population of the United States and Outlying Areas: 1940 to 1960. 2 pages. 1961.

4. Urban and Rural Population of the United States by States: 1960 and 1950. 4 pages. 1961.

5. Population of Urbanized Areas: 1960 and 1950. 12 pages. 1961.

6. Population of Cities of 10,000 or More, by Wards: 1960. 25 pages. 1961.

7. Rank of Cities of 100,000 or More: 1960. 3 pages. 1961.

8. Population of Cities of 10,000 or More: 1960. 7 pages. 1961.

9. Population of Towns and Other Minor Civil Divisions in the New England States: 1940 to 1960. 10 pages. 1961.

10. Race of the Population of the United States, by States: 1960. 3 pages. 1961.

11. Age of the Population of the United States by States: 1960. 8 pages. 1961.

12. Marital Status of the Population of the United
States, by States: 1960. 3 pages. 1961.

13. Household Relationship of the Population of the
United States, by States: 1960. 4 pages.
1961.

14. Population Counts and Selected Characteristics
for Guam, Virgin Islands, American Samoa, and
Canal Zone: 1960. 12 pages. 1960.

15. Population Counts and Selected Characteristics
for Puerto Rico: 1960. 11 pages. 1961.

16. Annexations and the Growth of Population in
Standard Metropolitan Statistical Areas: 1950
to 1960. 14 pages. 1962.

17. Employment Status, Weeks Worked, Occupations,
and Industry for the Population of the United
States: 1960. 20 pages. 1962.

18. Income of Families and Persons in the United
States. 9 pages. 1962.

19. Geographic Mobility of the Population of the
United States: April 1960. 3 pages. 1962.

20. School Enrollment and Educational Attainment
for the United States: 1960. 6 pages. 1962.

21. Children Ever Born to Women 15 to 44 Years Old,
for the United States: 1960. 3 pages. 1962.

22. Place of Work and Means of Transportation to
Work for the United States: 1960. 2 pages.
1962.

23. Households, Married Couples, and Families in
the United States: 1960. 4 pages. 1962.

24. Place of Birth of the Population of the United
States: 1960. 4 pages. 1962.

25. Age of the Population of the United States:
1960. 4 pages. 1962.

26. Population of Congressional Districts for 88th Congress, April 1, 1960. 5 pages. 1962.

27. Industry Group by Occupation. 8 pages. 1962.

28. Birthplace and Country of Origin: 1960. 6 pages. 1962.

29. School Enrollment of the Population of the United States: 1960. 13 pages. 1962.

30. Mobility of the Population, by Age: 1960. 6 pages. 1962.

31. Veterans in the United States: 1960. 5 pages. 1962.

32. Population of the United States by Single Years of Age: 1960. 4 pages. 1962.

33. Industry of the Experienced Civilian Labor Force: 1960. 9 pages. 1962.

34. Social and Economic Characteristics, for Puerto Rico: 1960. 14 pages. 1962.

35. Employment Status, Weeks Worked, and Year Last Worked: 1960. 14 pages. 1962.

36. Income in 1959 of the Population of the United States: 1960. 14 pages. 1962.

37. Educational Attainment of the Population of the United States: 1960. 12 pages. 1962.

38. Families in the United States: 1960. 12 pages. 1962.

39. Marital Status of the Population: 1960. 8 pages. 1962.

40. Occupation of the Experienced Civilian Labor Force and the Labor Reserve: 1960. 16 pages. 1962.

41. Place of Work and Means of Transportation to Work: 1960. 9 pages. 1963.

42. Fertility of the Population: 1960. 6 pages. 1963.

43. Low Income Families: 1960. 55 pages. 1964.

44. Family Income in Metropolitan Areas: 1960. 8 pages. 1964.

45. Size of Income, by Family Characteristics: 1960. 8 pages. 1964.

46. Subject Guide to 1960 Census Data for Negro Population. 4 pages. 1964.

47. Age of the Foreign Stock by Country of Origin. 12 pages. 1965.

48. Per Capita and Median Family Income in 1959, for States, Standard Metropolitan Statistical Areas, and Counties. 72 pages. 1965.

49. Distribution of the Negro Population. 5 pages. 1965.

50. Labor Reserve. 12 pages. 1965.

51. Marital Status and Age at First Marriage: 1960. 20 pages. 1965.

52. Negro Population, by County: 1960 and 1950. 64 pages. 1966.

53. 1960 Population of Congressional Districts for the 90th Congress. 10 pages. 1966.

54. Poverty Areas in the 100 Largest Metropolitan Areas. 24 pages. 1967.

55. Population Characteristics of Selected Ethnic Groups in the Five Southwestern States. 46 pages. 1968.

56. 1960: Population of Congressional Districts for the 91st Congress. 6 pages. 1966.

Indexes

Alphabetical Index of Occupations and Industries

1960
C 3.223:Ocl/960, revised C 3.223:Ocl/960-2
HA 201.1960.A45 A60-9227, rev. A60-9803
331.7
1960.275
Research Pubns. Film 1960 Reel 31
xxiv, 649 pages

The index lists industries and occupations alphabetically in two columns, nearly three hundred of them gleaned from earlier censuses. Industries are coded by the standard classification system.

Classified Index of Occupations and Industries

1960
C 3.223:Ocl/2
HA 201.1960.A46
331.7
1960.276
Research Pubns. Film 1960 Reel 31
xx, 383 pages

In contrast to the above index, in this one the industries are listed in classified order on the first 20 pages. Occupations, based on a three digit scheme, are listed in the order which has continued throughout later censuses.

Geographic Code Identification Scheme

1960
C 3.223/13:960/1
G 106 U514
1960.273
Research Pubns. Film 1960 Reel 30

This volume, which is organized by state, with pages separately numbered by state, provides the county and minor civil division for each named place, followed by enumeration district and other codings. At the end of each state listing is an alphabetical listing of place names and their codes.

1960
Notes

1960 Monograph Series

This series was sponsored by the Census Bureau and the Social Science
Research Council. Unlike the 1950 monographs which were also sponsored by these two agencies but were privately printed, several of
these monographs, the first five, were published by the U.S. Government Printing Office.

Changing Characteristics of the Negro Population
    Daniel O. Price. 1970. viii, 269 pages. LC A 68-7969
  C 3.30:N31

Education of the American People
    John K. Folger and Charles B. Nam. 1967. ix, 290 pages.
  LC A 66-7677
  C 3.30:Ed8

Income Distribution in the United States
    Herman P. Miller. 1966. viii, 306 pages. LC A 66-7107/r85
  C 3.30:In

People of Rural America
    Dale E. Hathaway, J. Allen Beegle, and W. Keith Bryant. 1969.
  ix, 289 pages. LC A68-7381
  C 3.30:R88

People of the United States in the 20th Century
    1971. xxxviii, 1046 pages. LC 72-609904
  C 3.30:P81

Published by the University of Chicago, Community and Family Study
Center:

Population Mobility Within the United States
    Henry S. Shryock, Jr. 1964. x, 470 pages. LC 73-174235

Contributions to Urban Sociology
    Ernest W. Burgess and Donald J. Bogue, Editors. 1964. xi, 673 pages
  LC 63-21309

Skid Row in American Cities
    Donald J. Bogue. 1963. xiv, 521 pages. LC 62-22329

THE UNITED STATES OF AMERICA

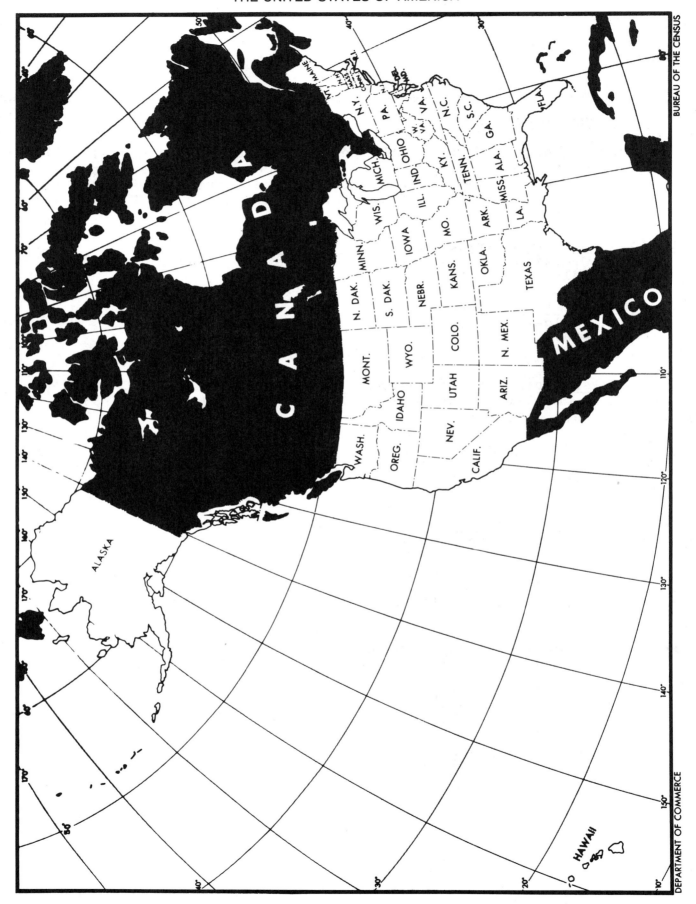

BUREAU OF THE CENSUS

DEPARTMENT OF COMMERCE

1970
POPULATION INFORMATION IN THE NINETEENTH DECENNIAL CENSUS

The grey and blue volumes of the 1970 Census continued the basic arrangement of the 1950 and 1960 Censuses. They are longer and more extensive and thus require a great deal more shelf space. Volume I is Characteristics of the Population, and Volume II is Subject Reports of which there are forty individual volumes. The 1970 Population Census, like all censuses since 1940, was accompanied by a Housing Census. Three sets of final unbound reports included data from both the population and the housing censuses: 241 Census Tract Reports, 523 Demographic Trends for Metropolitan Areas, and 76 Employment Profiles for Selected Low-Income Areas.

Volume I, Characteristics of the Population, Part A, Number of Inhabitants, contains the final population counts. Data for the United States and the states (alphabetically Alabama through Mississippi) are in Section 1; and Missouri through Wyoming, together with Puerto Rico and the outlying areas are in Section 2. These volumes are compilations of the PC(1)A reports, which were earlier issued unbound. Part A includes counts not only for the United States as a whole and the states, but for counties, Standard Metropolitan Areas, urbanized areas, county subdivisions, all incorporated places, as well as unincorporated places with a count of 1,000 persons.

In addition to the separate count of the population in Part A, Volume I also includes a two-section Characteristics of the Population with United States data, Parts 2 through 52 for the states and the District of Columbia, and parts 53 through 58 for Puerto Rico, Guam, the U.S. Virgin Islands, American Samoa, the Canal Zone and the Trust Territory of the Pacific Islands. Each of these parts includes data from the PC(1)A, "Number of Inhabitants"; PC(1)B, "General Population Characteristics"; PC(1)C "General Social and Economic Characteristics"; and PC(1)D "Detailed Characteristics" reports.

Volume II Subject Reports is divided into ten groups, similar to those of the 1960 Census: race, ethnic background and language, migration, families, marriages, education, employment, occupations and industries, income, low income and a final miscellaneous group. New in 1970 were volumes on work disability, persons of high income, and sources of family income.

The Census Tract Reports, PHC(1) reports, for the 241 Standard Metropolitan Statistical Areas include population characteristics as well as information from the housing census for each of the Census Tracts in those areas. A map of the tracts accompanies each report.

The series of General Demographic Trends for Metropolitan Area reports, designated PHC(2) reports, was published for each state, the District of Columbia and the United States. With some data for

counties and summarized data for the states as a whole, these reports
mainly concern population in the metropolitan areas and changes
between 1960 and 1970.

The 76 PHC(3) reports, <u>Employment Profiles of Selected Low-Income
Areas</u> cover 51 cities and 7 sets of rural counties together with a
<u>United States Summary</u>. Unlike other 1970 reports, this series re-
sulted a special questionnaire used in predetermined areas. Also published after the 1970 enumeration, were a number of <u>Supplementary Re-
ports</u> ranging in length from 3 to 75 pages on precise census subjects
such as voting age population and country of origin of the foreign
born. A number of lesser reports were published including an <u>Alpha-
betical Index</u> and a <u>Classified Index of Industries and Occupations</u>.

Considerable data were published only in microform as a result of the
1970 decennial enumeration. Other data were also made available on
computer tape. This volume is, however, intended only as a guide to
the printed volumes. Catalogs published by the Census Bureau should
be consulted for information on the microforms and computer tapes.

<u>Population Inquiries</u>

Inquiries as to age, sex, race, marital status and relationship to
the head of the household were continued as 100 percent questions.
In the case of sample questions, once a household was selected, all
members were included in the sample. Some sample questions were
asked at 15 percent of the households, some at 5 percent, and some at
both, for a total of 20 percent of the households. The 20 percent
items included inquiries as to place of birth, education, children
ever born, occupation, earnings and employment. The smaller samples
included questions on Spanish background, country of birth of father
and mother, naturalization, language, prior residence, current school
attendance, prior marriages, veteran status, vocational training,
disability and some employment inquiries.

Seventy million households received census questionnaires by mail in
1970. Those in large metropolitan areas, amounting to some 60 percent of the population, were asked to mail back the questionnaires.
In the remaining areas of the country, enumerators visited the household and collected the questionnaires, asking any of the sample
questions if the household was designated as one in the sample.

By 1970, the Census Bureau had developed FOSDIC - Film Optical Sen-
sing Device for Input to Computers. FOSDIC could scan the answers
written in small circles and transfer them to computer tape for
quick and accurate processing.

1970
MAJOR POPULATION VOLUMES OF THE NINETEENTH DECENNIAL CENSUS

VOLUME	TITLE

Volume I   Characteristics of the Population

Part A   Number of Inhabitants
         Section 1   United States,
                     Alabama-Mississippi
         Section 2   Missouri-Wyoming, Puerto
                     Rico and Outlying Areas

Part 1   United States Summary
         Section 1
         Section 2

Parts 2-58 - States and Outlying Areas

Volume II   Subject Reports

1 A   National Origin and Language
1 B   Negro Population
1 C   Persons of Spanish Origin
1 D   Persons of Spanish Surname
1 E   Puerto Ricans in the United States
1 F   American Indians
1 G   Japanese, Chinese and Filipinos in
      the United States

2 A   State of Birth
2 B   Mobility for States and the Nation
2 C   Mobility for Metropolitan Areas
2 D   Lifetime and Recent Migration
2 E   Migration between State Economic Areas

3 A   Women by Number of Children Ever Born
3 B   Childspacing and Current Fertility

4 A   Family Composition
4 B   Persons by Family Characteristics
4 C   Marital Status
4 D   Age at First Marriage
4 E   Persons in Institutions and Other Group
      Quarters

1970
Major Population Volumes

VOLUME	TITLE		
Volume II (continued)	5	A	School Enrollment
	5	B	Educational Attainment
	5	C	Vocational Training
	6	A	Employment Status and Work Experience
	6	B	Persons Not Employed
	6	C	Persons with Work Disability
	6	D	Journey to Work
	6	E	Veterans
	7	A	Occupational Characteristics
	7	B	Industrial Characteristics
	7	C	Occupation by Industry
	7	D	Government Workers
	7	E	Occupation and Residence in 1965
	7	F	Occupations of Persons with High Earnings
	8	A	Sources and Structure of Family Income
	8	B	Earnings by Occupation and Education
	8	C	Income of the Farm-Related Population
	9	A	Low-Income Population
	9	B	Low-Income Areas in Large Cities
	10	A	Americans Living Abroad
	10	B	State Economic Areas
Final Reports			Censuses of Population and Housing
			Census Tracts Reports 1-241
			General Demographic Trends for Metropolitan Areas, 1960 to 1970
			Employment Profiles of Selected Low-Income Areas

Notes on other publications of the 1970 Census that contain population information are provided at the end of the 1970 section.

Decennial Year	1970
Census	Nineteenth Decennial Census
Volume	Volume I Part A Sections 1 and 2

Title	1970 Census of Population
	Characteristics of the Population
	Number of Inhabitants
	Section 1 United States, Alabama-
	         Mississippi
	Section 2 Missouri-Wyoming, Puerto Rico
	         and Outlying Areas

Publication	Department of Commerce, Bureau of the Census Washington, DC: Government Printing Office
Date	1972

Classifications

Supt. of Documents	C 3.223/10:970/v.1/pt.A/sec. 1 and 2
Library of Congress	HA 201.1970.A568 v.1 pt.A sec. 1 and 2
card	72-60036
Dewey	312.0973
University of Texas	1970.1 and 1970.2

Microforms

Research Pubns.	Film 1970 Reel 1
A.S.I.	ASI 1974 2531-3
Pages	Sec. 1 xvi, 249 pages in the "U.S. Summary"; state pages separately numbered
Maps, illustrations	36 pages of colored maps and charts precede U.S. pages in Section 1; maps for each state.
Notes	These two bound volumes are compilations of the 58 PC(1)A reports by the same title which were issued in paper cover in 1970 and 1971 for each state, the District of Columbia, Puerto Rico and the outlying areas. The "U.S. Summary" chapter in Section 1 includes consid- erably more data than the state chapters.

1970
Volume I Characteristics of the Population Part A Sections 1 and 2

United States Summary Tables 1-46	United States	Regs., Divns., States	SMSAs, SCAs	Other

Demographic Characteristics

	United States	Regs., Divns., States	SMSAs, SCAs	Other
Aggregate population	1,8-10	8,10,14, 24	32-37, 42	24,28, 29,31, 34
Historic from 1790	2,8,9	8-10		28
Outlying areas				1
historic from 1950				1
Population abroad	1			
historic from 1950	1			
Puerto Rico				1,8-10, 24
Rank of states		14,15		
historic from 1920		14		
Standard Consolidated Areas			33	
Standard Metropolitan				
Statistical Areas			32,37	
historic from 1950			32	
inside/outside SMSAs			42	
constituent parts			34,41	
rank			36	
Urbanized areas				20
rank				21
Counties				24
historic from 1960				24
Cities of 100,000				28
historic from 1790				28
rank				28,29
50 largest				23
Places of 2,500				31
historic from 1960				31
Areas annexed since 1960				30,38- 40
Areas with special censuses since 1960				45
Economic Subregions				43
State Economic Areas				44
Congressional Districts				13

Apportionment, Geography

	United States	Regs., Divns., States	SMSAs, SCAs	Other
Apportionment	12	12		

1970
Volume I Characteristics of the Population Part A Sections 1 and 2

United States Summary Tables 1-46	United States	Regs., Divns., States	SMSAs, SCAs	Other
Density	2	11	35	20,31
Historic from 1920	11	11		
from 1960				20
By size of place	4,19			
Urban/rural	3,7,16	16	27,41	
Historic from 1790	3,7,18	18		
Incorporated & unincorporated places	6	17		
Historic from 1960	6			
Inside/outside SMSAs	5,17	17	34,41, 42	
Urbanized areas	4	16	16	20,21
Historic from 1960				20
County subdivisions, number & type	22	22		
By size	26	26		
By percent urban	24	27		
By percent change since 1960	25	25		
Places, number and type	23	23		
Census tracts, number in tracted areas				46

1970
Volume I   Characteristics of the Population   Part A   Sections 1 and 2

State and Outlying Area Tables 1-15	States	SMSAs	Counties	Other
Demographic Characteristics				
Aggregate population	1	13,14	9,10	6,7,10
Historic from earliest census	1			7
from 1960		13	10	6
Incorporated places of 10,000				7
historic from earliest census				7
Incorporated places and unin-				
corporated places of 1,000				6
County subdivisions			10	
Places				10
Urbanized areas				11,12
historic from 1960				11
Congressional districts	15			15
Apportionment, Geography				
Apportionment	15			
Density	9		9	
Size of place	2			
Historic from 1920	3			
By incorporated/unincorporated				
status	5			
Inside/outside SMSAs	4			
Urban/rural	1	14	9	
Historic from earliest census	1			
from 1920	3			
from 1960			9	
Congressional districts				15

Decennial Year	1970
Census	Nineteenth Decennial Census
Volume	Volume I Part 1 United States Summary
Title	1970 Census of Population Characteristics of the Population United States Summary Sections 1 and 2
Publication	Department of Commerce, Bureau of the Census Washington, DC: Government Printing Office
Date	1973

Classifications

Supt. of Documents	C 3.223/10:970/v.1/pt.1/sec. 1 and 2
Library of Congress	HA 201.1970.A568 v.1 pt.1 sec. 1 and 2
card	72-60036
Dewey	312.0973
University of Texas	1970.3 and 1970.4

Microforms

Research Pubns.	Film 1970 Reel 2
A.S.I.	ASI 1974 2531-1.1

Pages	Sec. 1 vi, 578; Sec. 2 iii, 579-1965, 79a pages
Maps, illustrations	Sec. 1 numerous colored maps and graphs, especially pp. 5-36 and 343-358; Sec. 2, maps.
Notes	Tables 1-188 are in Section 1 and Tables 189-371 are in Section 2. The table guides on the inside covers combine the two volumes. In this guide, however, there are separate table guides to the two sections on the fol- lowing pages.

1970
Volume I   Characteristics of the Population   Part 1   United States
Summary   Section 1   Tables 1-188

	United States	Regions, Divisions, States	SMSAs, SCAs, Ur.Areas, Places
Demographic Characteristics			
Aggregate population	1,8	8,24	
Historic from 1790	8-10	8-10	
Outlying areas	1,49		
Population abroad	1		
Congressional Districts		13	
States by rank		14,15	
Urbanized areas			20,21
Counties		24	24
Cities			28-31
historic from 1790			28
from 1850			29
Standard Metropolitan Statistical Areas			32,34-39
Standard Consolidated Areas			33
Economic Subregions			43
State Economic Areas			44
Areas with special censuses since 1960			45
Age	47,49-53, 85	56,57,62, 63,130	
Single years	50,51, 107,124	56,61, 130,141	
Historic from 1880	51		
By sex	49,50,52		
Race	50,52,53, 68,69,71, 74-79,81-95,118-129	55-63, 131-135, 142	66,67
By sex	50-53	55-57	
historic from 1900	48		
by age	50,52		
Spanish origin	85,86,90, 118-129		

1970
Volume I   Characteristics of the Population   Part 1   United States
Summary   Section 1   Tables 1-188

	United States	Regions, Divisions, States	SMSAs, SCAs, Ur.Areas, Places
Sex	48	57,61-63	66,67
Historic from 1900	48		
By age	48		
By race	49		
Marital status	47,54,89, 90,101, 112	58,59,64, 132	66

Social and Economic Characteristics

	United States	Regions, Divisions, States	SMSAs, SCAs, Ur.Areas, Places
Disabilities	89,100, 111	160	
Education			
School enrollment	73,74,88, 99,110, 119,125	131,137, 140,154, 155	
historic from 1910	73		
Years of school completed	75,88,99, 100,110, 111,119, 125	131,137, 140,156, 157	
In college in 1970	149	149	
Vocational training	88,99,110		
Employment/unemployment	77,79,90, 93,99, 101,103, 110,112, 113,120	132,137, 141	
Place of work	87,98,109	132,137,151	
Class of employer	80,93,104, 115,120, 126	133,173,174	

	United States	Regions, Divisions, States	SMSAs, SCAs, Ur.Areas, Places
Families	54,83-85, 89,94-96, 100,108, 111,118, 119,124, 125	58,130,135, 136,139,140, 159,182	
Unrelated individuals	54,85,94- 96,105, 106,123	58,65,130, 135,139, 180-182	
Fertility	47,76,89, 100,111, 119,125	131,136, 140,158	66
Households	47,54,85, 89,95,96, 106,107, 118,123, 124,129	58,65,130, 139,140, 182	66
Group quarters	47,54,85, 89,96, 100,107, 111,118	58,65,130, 160	66
Housing		139,150	
Income	83,84,94, 105,116, 121,122, 127,128	135,139, 141,178- 181	
Industry	80,82,92, 103,114, 122,128	134,138,141, 169-172	
Institutional population	54,85,87, 89,90,96, 107,111, 118,124	58,65,130, 132,139, 149,160	

1970
Volume I Characteristics of the Population Part 1 United States
Summary Section 1 Tables 1-188

	United States	Regions, Divisions, States	SMSAs, SCAs, Ur.Areas, Places
Labor force	77,78,90, 101,112, 120,126	132,137,139, 141,161,162, 164	
Language Mother tongue	86,108	140,146,147	
Migration/mobility	72,87,98, 109,119, 125	131,137,140, 143,148,149	
Military/veterans	1,49,71, 87,90,98, 100,101, 109	149,150, 153,160	
Nativity	68,86, 108	136,140,143	
Place of birth	69,87,98, 119,125	131,136,143	
Specific by country of origin	70,86,97, 98,108	136,144,145	
Parentage	68,86		
Occupations	81,91,93, 94,102, 113,121, 127	133,138, 165-168	
Last occupation of unemployed	93,104, 115,122, 128		
Poverty	95,106, 117,123, 129	135,139,182	
Transportation	87,98,109	132,152	

1970
Volume I   Characteristics of the Population   Part 1   United States
Summary   Section 1   Tables 1-188

	United States	Regions, Divisions, States	SMSAs, SCAs, Ur.Areas, Places
Apportionment, Geography			
Apportionment	12	12	
Density	2	11	20
Urban/rural	3,7,16, 17,47	16,17	31,35,41
Historic from 1790	3,7,18	18	
Age	50,52,61, 85,96		
Race	48,52,61, 118,119	142	
Spanish origin	118,119		
Sex	52,96		
Marital status	54,89,90, 101,120		
Education	73-75,88, 99,100,111, 119		
Employment	88,90,93, 101,104,112, 120		
Family	54,85,89, 94,96,100, 119,122,123		
Households	85,95,96, 100,106,118		
Income	84,94,105, 122,139		
Industry	80,82,138		
Institutional population	54,85,89, 96,100,118		
Labor force	90,101,120		
Language	86,97		
Migration/mobility	72,87,119		
Military/veterans	71,87		
Nativity	68,86,87, 97,98,108, 119,136		

1970
Volume I Characteristics of the Population Part 1 United States
Summary Section 1 Tables 1-188

	United States	Regions, Divisions, States	SMSAs, SCAs, Ur.Areas, Places
Urban/rural (continued)			
Occupations	91,93,94, 102,104, 105,121, 122,138, 139		
Poverty	95,106, 123		
Transportation	87,98		
Farm/nonfarm	53,85,86, 90,98		
Size of place	4,19,54, 96,106	19	
Inside/outside metropolitan areas	5,46,47	42	
Metropolitan/nonmetropolitan residence	107		
Standard Metropolitan Statistical Areas	38-40		
Counties, number	25-27		
County subdivisions, number	22		
Places, number and type	23		
Incorporated/unincorporated places	6		
Census tracts, number	46		
Economic Subregions	43	43	

1970
Volume I Characteristics of the Population Part 1 United States
Summary Section 2 Tables 189-371

	United States	Regions, Divisions, States	SMSAs, SCAs, Ur.Areas, Places
Demographic Characteristics			
Marital status	203,210, 211,331, 336	279,284, 331,336	351
Social and Economic Characteristics			
Citizenship			
Native, alien, naturalized, by age and sex	194,195	273	
Disabilities			
Noninstitutional population 16 to 64 years with work disabilities			
by length of disability	220	292,343	362
by characteristics	220		
Education			
School enrollment			
by single years of age 3-34	326	326	
by level school	197	275	
by employment	217	289	
percent enrolled in labor force			358,359
by poverty status	267		
Years of school completed	199,328, 329,344	276,328, 329,344	349,350, 365
by persons not enrolled	198,327		
by income	249,254, 344	344	365
by labor force participation	209		354
by occupation	231		
by poverty status	263,268		
vocational training	200,201	277,278	

1970
Volume I   Characteristics of the Population   Part 1   United States
Summary   Section 2   Tables 189-371

	United States	Regions, Divisions, States	SMSAs, SCAs, Ur.Areas, Places
Employment/unemployment	215	287	360,361
By age	215	287	
percent employed, by sex	341,342	341,342	360,361
By school enrollment	217	289	
Of families	253	310	
By income	247,248	310	
By poverty status	261,262	316,317	
Hours worked	217	289	
Weeks worked	218,247	290,317	
by industry	237		
by occupation	224		
by earnings	247	305	
Place of work	242,243		363
Unemployed	215,261	287,316	
year last worked	219,224, 237	291	
Class employer	225,238, 243	295,300	
Families	204,206, 207	282,283	353
By relationship	204	280	
By size	208	308	
By number, presence of children	333,334	333,334	
Persons per family	208		
By education	209,254		354
By labor force participation	209	310	354
By income	250-257	307-312	366
By number earners	252	309	
By poverty level	259-267	314-321	368,371
Farmers, farms	257	312	
Fertility	212-214, 337	285,286, 337	
Households	204,205	280	367
By size	258	313,346	367
Head of household, by sex	258	313	367
Group quarters	205	281,332	352

1970
Volume I   Characteristics of the Population   Part 1   United States
Summary   Section 2   Tables 189-371

	United States	Regions, Divisions, States	SMSAs, SCAs, Ur.Areas, Places
Immigration			
Year of immigration	195		
Income			
Of persons	244-246	303,304	365
by employment status	248		
by family status	246		
by education	249	306,344	365
by earnings	247	305	
Of families	250-257, 345	307-312, 345	366
by education	254		
Of households	258	313,346	367
Of unrelated individuals	250,257, 258	307,309, 312,313, 346	
Earnings	227-229, 240,241, 243,253	296,297, 301,303, 305,310	
Industry	229,235-241,257	298-302	
Institutional population	205,206	281,282, 332	352
Labor force	209,219	288,291, 335,338-340	354-359
Status of husband/wife	209,335	335	
Migration/mobility	191,196, 230,234, 325	274,324, 325	
Military/veterans	202,330	330	
Veterans by period of service	202		
Armed forces	205,215, 230	287	

1970
Volume I   Characteristics of the Population   Part 1   United States
Summary   Section 2   Tables 189-371

	United States	Regions, Divisions, States	SMSAs, SCAs, Ur.Areas, Places
Nativity	192,195, 272		
General nativity	189-191, 322,323	269-271, 322-324	348,369, 370
Specific, by country of birth	192	272	
Foreign born by mother tongue	193		
Occupations	221-224, 226,232-234	293,294	
Poverty	347	347	
Transportation	242		364

Apportionment, Geography

Urban/rural
  Education
    school enrollment   217,267
    years of school completed   198,199,249,
                                     263,268
  Employment   215,217-219,
                                     248,253,261,
                                     262
  Families   206-209,250-
                                     253,255,257-
                                     259,266
  Fertility   212,214
  Households   204,205,258
  Income   245-253,255,
                                     257,258
  Institutional population   205,206
  Labor force   216,219
  Occupations   222,255,262
  Poverty   259-268

Decennial Year	1970
Census	Nineteenth Decennial Census
Volume	Volume I Parts 2 through 58
Title	1970 Census of Population Characteristics of the Population States and Outlying Areas
Publication	Department of Commerce, Bureau of the Census Washington, DC: Government Printing Office
Date	1973

Classifications

Supt. of Documents	C 3.223/10:970/v.1/pts.2-58
Library of Congress	HA 201.1970.A568 v.1 pts.2-58
card	72-60036
Dewey	312.0973
University of Texas	1970.5 through 1970.65

Microforms

Research Pubns.	Film 1970 Reels 3 through 39
A.S.I.	ASI 1974 2531.2 through 2531.54
Pages	Vary
Maps, illustrations	Maps and graphs in each of the 4 chapters.
Notes	These reports were published first in paper covers as PC(1)A, PC(1)B, PC(1)C, and PC(1)D. Each part includes four appendices at the end of the tables with definitions of the terminology used as well as explanations of census geography. Separate reprts were published for Puerto Rico, Guam, the Virgin Islands, American Samoa, the Canal Zone and the Trust Territory of the Pacific Islands.

1970
Volume I Characteristics of the Population Parts 2-58 States and Outlying Areas

	State	SMSAs	Counties	Places
Demographic Characteristics				
Aggregate Population	1	13,14, 23,40		6-8,10, 23,40
Historic from earliest census	1	13		
from 1900				7
from 1960			9,10	6
Incorporated places				6
areas annexed since 1960				8
Incorporated places of 10,000				7
Unincorporated place of 1,000				6
County subdivisions			10,33	
Urbanized areas		11,12		
Congressional Districts	15			
Age	16,19-21, 48,59, 138,156	24,96, 138,156	35,38, 129,134, 136	16,24, 29-33, 96,112
Single years, by sex	19			
Historic from 1900	21			
Race	16-18	16,23, 24	16,34, 35,38, 134,136	24,27, 31-33
Note that the following tables are for Negro population only: 91-94,108-111,125-128,181				
White, Negro, Indian, Japanese, Chinese, Filipino, Other	17,18	23	34	23
by sex, historic from 1900	17,18			
by age	139			
Korean	139			
Spanish heritage	139,140, 147, 156-159	169,182		
Note that data vary among states, and that Tables 96-101, 112-116,129-133,182 are for Spanish heritage only.				

1970
Volume I Characteristics of the Population Parts 2-58 States
and Outlying Areas

	State	SMSAs	Counties	Places
Sex	17-20	23	34,35,38	23,24, 27,28, 31-33
By age	21	24	35	24
by race	20	24	35	24
historic from 1900	17			
Marital status	16,22, 152,155, 165	16,26, 152,155	16,37	16,26, 30
Couples with/without own household		40	43	40

Social and Economic Characteristics

	State	SMSAs	Counties	Places
Citizenship	143,144	143,144		
Disabilities				
Unable to work, 16-64 years	52,63, 169	74,84, 169		84
Education				
School enrollment	45,51, 62,146, 166,215	40,83, 91,97, 146,166, 215	43,120, 125,130	40,42, 83,91, 97,103, 108,113, 117,130
Vocational education	51,62, 149,150	73,83		
Years of school completed	46,51, 62,147	73,83, 97,146, 147	120,125, 130,134, 136	40,91, 97,108, 113,117, 147
by age	52,63, 148	74,84, 148	120	103
by head of family	158	158		
by income	197,202	197,202		
by occupation	179			
by poverty status	211,216	211,216		

1970
Volume I Characteristics of the Population Parts 2-58 States
and Outlying Areas

	State	SMSAs	Counties	Places
Employment/unemployment	46,53,64	41,75, 85,92, 98	121,126, 131,135, 137	41,85, 92,98, 104,109, 114,117
By age	164,168	164,168		
By education	62,166	83,92, 98,166		104,114, 117
By income	196,201	196,201		
By poverty status	209	209		
Hours worked	166	166		
Weeks worked in 1969	46,56,67, 167,172, 185,195, 201,210	88,92, 98,167, 172,185, 195.201	121,126, 131	88,92, 98,104, 109,114, 117
Year last worked	168,172, 185	168,172, 185		
By place of work	50,61, 191	82,190	119	82,102
By class of employer	173,186	88,92, 98,173, 186	121,126, 131	92,98, 104,109, 114,118
Families	22,48,52, 59,63, 155-158	22,48, 52,59, 63,70, 84,91, 97,155-158	36,120, 125,129, 130	29,84, 91,97, 103,108, 112,113
By race	91	91,97		
By characteristics of head	158	158		
Subfamilies	52,63,155	84,155	120,125	103,108
Unrelated individuals	22,48,59, 153,155, 198,200, 205,207, 213	25,26, 96,153, 155, 198, 200,205, 207,213	36-38, 129,134, 136	29-31, 112
Fertility	45,52,63	84,91, 97	43,120, 125,134, 136	84,91, 103,113

122

1970
Volume I Characteristics of the Population Parts 2-58 State
and Outlying Areas

	State	SMSAs	Counties	Places
Households	16,22,39, 48,59,70, 153	16,25, 26,96	16,33, 36-39, 134,136	16,25, 26,29- 33,39, 96,112
By age of head	22	25	36	25,29
Group quarters	16,22, 39,52, 63,154	16,84, 154	16,36-38, 120	16,29- 33,39, 84
Immigration - year	144	144		
Income - for 1969	47,57, 68,192- 194,198- 200	41,89, 94,99, 100, 192-194, 198-200	44,88, 124,128, 133,135, 137	41,42, 94,99, 100,107, 111,116, 118
Families and unrelated individuals	198-205	89,94, 198-204		89,94
Persons	192-197	192-197		
Households	206	206		
Earnings	57,68, 175-177, 188,189, 191,195, 201	89,93, 99,175, 176,188, 189,195, 201	122,127, 132	89,99, 105,110, 115
Industry	47,55, 66,177, 180-189, 204	87,94, 100, 180, 184-189, 204	123,127, 132,134, 136, 204	87,94, 100,106, 110,115, 117
Institutional population	22,48,52, 59,61,63, 154,155	25,26, 84,96, 154,155	36-38, 120,129, 134,136	25,26, 29-31, 103,112
Labor force	46,53,64, 158,165	85,92, 98,158, 165	44,121, 126,131, 135,137	41,42, 85,98, 104,109, 114,117

1970
Volume I Characteristics of the Population Parts 2-58 States
and Outlying Areas

	State	SMSAs	Counties	Places
Language - Mother tongue	48,49,60, 71,142, 153	40,81	119	40,81, 102
Migration/mobility				
State of residence/place of birth	45,61	40,82, 91	43,130	40,42, 82,91, 102,108, 113,116
Residence in 1965	45,50,61, 72,140, 145	82,91	119,125, 130	82,97, 102,113, 117
Year moved into present house	50,61,72	82		
Military/veterans	50,61,72, 151	82	119	82,102
Nativity				
General nativity	45,138- 140	40,81, 91,97, 138	43,119, 125,130	40,42, 81,91, 97,102, 108,113, 117
Specific nativity				
foreign born by country of birth	49,60	81,144		144
foreign stock by country of origin	45,60,141		119	102
Occupations	46,54,65, 170-182, 210	76,86, 88,93, 94,99, 171-176, 180,203, 210	122,123, 127,132, 135,137	86,93, 105,110, 115,118
Last occupation of unemployed		88,94, 100	123	88,94, 100,106
Poverty	58,69, 207-216	90,95, 101, 207-216	124,128, 133,135, 137	90,95, 101

1970
Volume I Characteristics of the Population Parts 2-58 States and Outlying Areas

	State	SMSA	Counties	Places
Transportation to work	50,61,72	82,190		82

Apportionment, Geography

Size of place	2,59,70			
Historic from 1920	3			
Incorporated/unincorporated	5			
Urban/rural	1	9		
Historic from earliest census	1			
Age	20,59,138			
Race	17,18,48			
Marital status	20,22,52, 155,165			
Disabilities	52,53,63			
Education	51,52,62, 146,147, 166,215			
Employment	51,53,56,64, 164,166,168, 196,201,209			
Families	22,48,52, 59,63,153, 155,156			
Households	22,48,52, 59,63,153, 154,197			
Income	57,68, 192-201,205			
Industry	55,66			
Institutional population	22,48,52, 59,63			
Labor force	53,64, 158,165			
Language	49,60			
Migration/mobility	50,61			
Military/veterans	50,61			
Occupations	54,56,65, 67,171,210			
Poverty	211,216	154,155		
Transportation	50,61			

Decennial Year	1970
Census	Nineteenth Decennial Census
Volume	Volume II Subject Reports Part 1
Titles	1970 Census of Population 1 A National Origin and Language 1 B Negro Population 1 C Persons of Spanish Origin 1 D Persons of Spanish Surname 1 E Puerto Ricans in the United States 1 F American Indians 1 G Japanese, Chinese, and Filipinos in the United States
Publication	Department of Commerce, Bureau of the Census Washington, DC: Government Printing Office
Date	1973

Classifications

Supt. of Documents	C 3.223/10:970/v.2/pts.1 A, B, C, D, E, F, G
Library of Congress	HA 201.1970.A568 v.2 pts.1 A, B, C, D, E. F, G
card	72-60036
Dewey	312.0973
University of Texas	1970.66 through 1970.72

Microforms

Research Pubns.	Film 1970 Reel 40
A.S.I.	ASI 1974 1 A 2533-27; 1 B 2533-14; 1 C 2533-21; 1 D 2533-25; 1 E 2533-33; 1 F 2533-20; 1 G 2533-28
Pages	1 A xi, 505, 21a; 1 B x, 2077, 24a; 1 C x, 199, 24a; 1 D vii, 122, 24a; 1 E xi, 123, 24a; 1 F xvi, 192, 24a; 1 G xi, 181, 24a pages
Maps, illustrations	Part 1 F has 2 maps.
Notes	Part 1 F includes a list of tribal groups.

1970
Volume II   Subject Reports   Parts 1 A, B, C, D, E, F and G

	A	B	C	D	E	F	G
				Part			

Demographic Characteristics

	A	B	C	D	E	F	G
Aggregate population	x	x	x			x	
Limited to persons of Puerto Rican birth or parentage in the U.S.					x		
Age	x	x	x	x	x	x	x
Race	x	x	x	x	x	x	x
Negroes		x					
American Indians						x	
Japanese, Chinese and Filipinos							x
Spanish origin			x				
Spanish surname - Limited to persons in 5 southwestern states					x		
Sex	x	x	x	x	x	x	x
Marital status	x	x	x	x	x	x	x

Social and Economic Characteristics

	A	B	C	D	E	F	G
Citizenship	x		x				
Education							
School enrollment	x	x	x	x	x	x	x
Years of school completed	x	x	x	x	x	x	x
Vocational training			x				
Employment/unemployment	x	x	x	x	x	x	x
Families	x	x	x	x	x	x	x
Fertility	x	x			x	x	x
Households	x	x	x	x	x	x	x
Group quarters	x	x	x	x	x		x
Housing		x	x	x	x		x
Whether living on reservation						x	

1970
Volume II Subject Reports   Parts 1 A, B, C, D, E, F and G

	A	B	C	Part D	E	F	G
Immigration	X						
Income	X	X	X	X	X	X	X
Industry		X	X	X	X	X	X
Institutional population	X	X	X	X	X		X
Labor force	X	X	X	X	X	X	X
Language						X	
Mother tongue	X			X	X		
Spanish language	X			X	X		
Migration/mobility	X	X	X	X	X	X	X
Nativity							
General nativity	X	X	X	X	X		X
Specific nativity by country of origin	X						
Mexico				X			
Parentage	X			X			
native/foreign/mixed	X			X			
Mexican/Puerto Rican/Cuban			X				
Occupations	X	X	X	X	X	X	X
Poverty	X	X	X	X	X	X	X
Transportation		X		X	X	X	X

Apportionment, Geography

	A	B	C	Part D	E	F	G
Urban/rural		X	X	X	X		X
Farm/nonfarm		X	X	X	X		X
Regions, Census Divisions	X	X	X		X		X
States		X	X	X	X		X
Standard Metropolitan Statistical Areas	X	X	X	X	X		X
Places		X	X	X			X

Decennial Year	1970
Census	Nineteenth Decennial Census
Volume	Volume II Subject Reports Part 2
Titles	1970 Census of Population 2 A State of Birth 2 B Mobility for States and the Nation 2 C Mobility for Metropolitan Areas 2 D Lifetime and Recent Migration 2 E Migration Between State Economic Areas
Publication	Department of Commerce, Bureau of the Census Washington, DC: Government Printing Office
Date	1973
Classifications	
Supt. of Documents	C 3.223/10:970/v.2/pts.2 A, B, C, D, E
Library of Congress	HA 201.1970.A568 v.2 pts.2 A, B, C, D, E
card	72-60036
Dewey	312.0973
University of Texas	1970.73 through 1970.77
Microforms	
Research Pubns.	Film 1970 Reels 41 and 42
A.S.I.	ASI 1974 2 A 2533-8; 2 B 2533-24; 2 C 2533-11; 2 D 2533-5; 2 E 2533-1
Pages	2 A viii, 277, 14a; 2 B xi, 422, 24a; 2 C xv, 424, 20a; 2 D viii, 521, 21a; 2 E 375, 21a pages
Maps, illustrations	One or two maps in each part.
Notes	Each report contains demographic data. Reports 2 B, C and D also contain socioeconomic data.

1970
Volume II   Subject Reports   Parts 2 A, B, C, D and E

	A	B	Part C	D	E
Demographic Characteristics					
Aggregate population	x		x		
Limited to persons 5+ years		x	x	x	x
Age	x	x	x	x	x
Race	x	x		x	x
Spanish origin, heritage	x			x	
Sex	x	x	x	x	x
Marital status		x			
Social and Economic Characteristics					
Education					
School enrollment		x		x	
college enrollment		x			
Years of school completed		x	x	x	
Employment/unemployment		x	x	x	
Families		x	x	x	
Fertility		x	x	x	
Households		x			
Group quarters		x			
Housing		x			
Income		x	x	x	
Institutional population		x			
Labor force		x	x		
Language					
Family head/Spanish language			x		

1970
Volume II   Subject Reports   Parts 2 A, B, C, D and E

	A	B	Part C	D	E
Migration/mobility	x	x	x	x	x
State of birth/region of residence	x				
Military/veterans		x	x		
Nativity					
General nativity	x				
State/region of birth	x	x			
Puerto Rican birth	x			x	
Occupations		x	x	x	
Poverty				x	
Apportionment, Geography					
Regions, Census Divisions		x		x	
State		x		x	
Standard Metropolitan Statistical Areas	x		x		
State Economic Areas					x
Size of place	x				

Decennial Year	1970
Census	Nineteenth Decennial Census
Volume	Volume II Subject Reports Part 3
Titles	1970 Census of Population 3 A Women by Number of Children Ever Born 3 B Childspacing and Current Fertility
Publication	Department of Commerce, Bureau of the Census Washington, DC: Government Printing Office
Date	3 A 1973; 3 B 1975

Classifications

Supt. of Documents	C 3.223/10:970/v.2/pts.3 A, B
Library of Congress	HA 201.1970.A568 v.2 pts.3 A, B
card	72-60036
Dewey	312.0973
University of Texas	1970.77 and 1977.78

Microforms

Research Pubns.	Film 1970 Reel 42 (3 A only)
A.S.I.	3 A ASI 1974 2533-36; 3 B ASI 1975 2533-40
Pages	3 A xvii, 379, 25a; 3 B xxix, 463, 22a pages
Maps, illustrations	One or two maps in each part.
Notes	These reports provide information comparable to that in the subject reports of the 1960 Census and to one report in the 1950 Census.

1970
Volume II Subject Reports Parts 3 A and B

	Part A	Part B
Demographic Characteristics		
Aggregate population		
Limited to women 15+ years	x	x
Age		
Limited to women 15+ years.		
Differences, husband and wife	x	x
Of mother, at birth of first child		x
Race	x	x
American Indians by tribe	x	
Spanish origin	x	x
Sex	x	x
Of children		x
Marital status	x	x
Presence/absence of spouse	x	x
Social and Economic Characteristics		
Disabilities	x	
Education	x	x
Of husband and wife		x
Families	x	
Farmers/farms	x	x
Fertility	x	x
Children ever born	x	x
Single sons and daughters	x	
Households	x	
Relationship of mother to head	x	x
Group quarters	x	x
Presence/absence of children in household		x
Income	x	x

1970
Volume II Subject Reports Parts 3 A and B

	Part A	Part B
Institutional population	x	
Labor force status	x	x
Migration/mobility	x	
Nativity		
General nativity	x	x
Specific, by country of birth	x	
Occupations	x	x
Poverty status		x
Apportionment, Geography		
Regions		x
Metropolitan/nonmetropolitan	x	x
Urbanized areas	x	x
Lower-income areas of cities	x	x
Urban/rural	x	x
Rural farm/nonfarm	x	x
Vital Statistics		
Births	x	x
Marriages	x	x

Decennial Year	1970
Census	Nineteenth Decennial Census
Volume	Volume II Subject Reports Part 4
Titles	1970 Census of Population 4 A Family Composition 4 B Persons by Family Characteristics 4 C Marital Status 4 D Age at First Marriage 4 E Persons in Institutions and Other Group Quarters
Publication	Department of Commerce, Bureau of the Census Washington, DC: Government Printing Office
Date	4 C 1972; 4 A, B, D, E 1973
Classifications	
Supt. of Documents	C 3.223/10:970/v.2/pts.4 A, B, C, D, E
Library of Congress	HA 201.1970.A568 v.2 pts.4 A, B, C, D, E
card	72-60036
Dewey	312.0973
University of Texas	1970.79 through 1970.83
Microforms	
Research Pubns.	Film 1970 Reels 42 and 43
A.S.I.	ASI 1974 4 A 2533-17; 4 B 2533-12; 4 C 2533-4; 4 D 2533-15; 4 E 2533-32
Pages	4 A ix, 298, 24a; 4 B ix, 168, 21a; 4 C ix, 299, 21a; 4 D ix, 277, 20a; 4 E xiv, 518, 21a pages
Maps, illustrations	One or two maps in each part.
Notes	Introductory pages provide precise information on comparability of data in earlier censuses on the subjects covered in these reports.

1970
Volume II Subject Reports Parts 4 A, B, C, D and E

	A	B	Part C	D	E
Demographic Characteristics					
Aggregate population					x
Age	x	x	x	x	x
Limited to persons 14 to 79 years				x	
Race	x	x	x	x	x
Spanish origin	x	x	x	x	x
Sex	x	x	x	x	x
Marital status	x	x	x	x	x
Presence/absence of spouse	x	x	x		
Social and Economic Characteristics					
Disabilities					x
Education	x	x	x	x	x
Employment		x		x	
Resident employee in household	x				
Families	x	x			
Parents/grandchildren/subfamilies	x				
Unrelated persons in household	x	x			
Presence/absence of children	x				
Farmers/farms	x	x			
Fertility		x			
Households	x	x			
Unrelated persons sharing living quarters		x			
Head of household living alone		x			
Housing					
Tenure	x				
Income	x	x	x	x	x

1970
Volume II   Subject Reports   Parts 4 A, B, C, D and E

	A	B	Part C	D	E
Institutional population		x			x
By type and size of institution					x
Labor force	x		x		
Migration/mobility	x				x
Military/veterans	x	x			x
Nativity					
General nativity	x		x	x	x
Parental nativity			x		
Foreign stock, by ethnic group	x				
Specific nativity, by country of origin			x	x	
Puerto Rican birth					x
Occupations	x	x	x	x	x

Apportionment, Geography

	A	B	C	D	E
Regions	x	x	x		
Urban/rural	x	x	x	x	x
Rural farm/nonfarm	x	x	x	x	x
Urbanized areas	x	x	x	x	
Central cities	x	x	x	x	
Urban fringe			x	x	

Vital Statistics

	A	B	C	D	E
Marriages					
Year of first marriage	x	x	x	x	
Years since first marriage					x
Marital history		x	x		
Times married		x			

Decennial Year	1970
Census	Nineteenth Decennial Census
Volume	Volume II Subject Reports Part 5
Titles	1970 Census of Population 5 A School Enrollment 5 B Educational Attainment 5 C Vocational Training
Publication	Department of Commerce, Bureau of the Census Washington, DC: Government Printing Office
Date	1973

Classifications

Supt. of Documents	C 3.223/10:970/v.2/pts.5 A, B, C
Library of Congress	HA 201.1970.A568 v.2 pts.5 A, B, C
card	72-60036
Dewey	312.0973
University of Texas	1970.84 through 1970.86

Microforms

Research Pubns.	Film 1970 Reel 43
A.S.I.	ASI 1974 5 A 2533-13; 5 B 2533-7; 5 C 2533-19
Pages	5 A xi, 344, 21a; 5 B x, 252, 21a; 5 C vii, 226, 21a pages
Maps, illustrations	One map each in Parts 5 A and B.
Notes	Educational attainment was first used as a question in 1940, replacing a question on literacy which had been used since 1840. It has been continued through 1980 in conjunction with question on school enrollment. This is the first use, in 1970, of a question on vocational training.

1970
Volume II Subject Reports Parts 5 A, B and C

	Part A	Part B	Part C
Demographic Characteristics			
Aggregate population			
Limited to persons 3-49 years	x		
Limited to persons 14+ years		x	
Limited to persons 16+ years			x
Age	x	x	x
Race	x	x	x
Spanish language, origin	x		x
Sex	x	x	x
Marital status	x	x	
Social and Economic Characteristics			
Citizenship	x		
Education			
School enrollment	x		
by type of school	x		
by control of school	x		
persons not enrolled	x		
college enrollment	x		
Years of school completed		x	x
by father/mother	x		
vocational school			x
Employment		x	x
Families	x	x	
Income	x	x	x
Industry			x
Labor force	x	x	x
Migration/mobility	x	x	

1970
Volume II Subject Reports Parts 5 A, B and C

	Part A	Part B	Part C
Military/veterans			x
Nativity			
General nativity	x	x	
Native born by region of birth	x	x	
Foreign born			
Mexican	x		
European, by country	x		
by country of birth	x		
Parentage		x	
Occupations	x	x	x
Of father	x		
Apportionment, Geography			
Regions	x		
Urbanized areas		x	
Urban/rural	x	x	
Farm/nonfarm	x		

Decennial Year	1970
Census	Nineteenth Decennial Census
Volume	Volume II Subject Reports Part 6
Titles	1970 Census of Population 6 A Employment Status and Work Experience 6 B Persons Not Employed 6 C Persons with Work Disability 6 D Journey to Work 6 E Veterans
Publication	Department of Commerce, Bureau of the Census Washington, DC: Government Printing Office
Date	1973

Classifications

Supt. of Documents	C 3.223/10:970/v.2/pts.6 A, B, C, D, E
Library of Congress	HA 201.1970.A568 v.2 pts.6 A, B, C, D, E
card	72-60036
Dewey	312.0973
University of Texas	1970.87 through 1970.91

Microforms

Research Pubns.	Film 1970 Reels 44 and 45
A.S.I.	ASI 1974 6 A 2533-16; 6 B 2533-34; 6 C 2533-10; 6 D 2533-39; 6 E 2533-29
Pages	6 A xi, 421, 21a; 6 B xx, 242, 21a; 6 C v, 174, 21a; 6 D xvii, 1132, 21a; 6 E ix, 199, 24a pages
Maps, illustrations	One map each in Parts 6 D and E.
Notes	Each of the reports in this group provides demographic data as well as a number of social and economic characteristics of those employed, those disabled, and of veterans.

1970
Volume II Subject Reports Parts 6 A, B, C, D and E

	A	B	Part C	D	E
Demographic Characteristics					
Aggregate population					
Limited to persons 14+ years	x	x			
Limited to persons 16+ years				x	
Limited to persons 18+ years			x		
Limited to male veterans					x
Age	x	x	x	x	x
Race	x	x	x	x	x
Spanish origin, language	x	x	x	x	x
Sex	x	x	x	x	
Limited to males					x
Marital status	x	x		x	x
Social and Economic Characteristics					
Disabilities					
Partial/complete			x		
Education					
School enrollment	x	x			
college enrollment		x			x
Years of school completed	x	x	x		x
Vocational school			x		
Employment/unemployment	x	x	x	x	x
Hours, weeks worked	x				x
Place of work				x	
Year last worked		x			
Families	x		x		
Fertility	x				
Households	x	x		x	x
Group quarters				x	x

1970
Volume II   Subject Reports   Parts 6 A, B, C, D and E

	Part A	B	C	D	E
Housing					x
Immigration/outmigration					x
Income	x	x	x	x	x
Industry		x		x	
Institutional population					x
Labor force	x		x		x
Labor reserve		x			
Migration/mobility	x				x
Military/veterans	x		x		
Period of service					x
Armed services 1965					x
Occupations		x	x	x	x
Poverty		x			
Transportation					
Place of residence/place of work				x	
Means of transportation				x	

Apportionment, Geography

	A	B	C	D	E
Standard Metropolitan Statistical Areas				x	
Urbanized areas	x	x	x		
Urban/rural	x	x	x		
Farm/nonfarm	x	x	x		

Decennial Year	1970
Census	Nineteenth Decennial Census
Volume	Volume II Subject Reports Part 7
Titles	1970 Census of Population
	7 A Occupational Characteristics
	7 B Industrial Characteristics
	7 C Occupation by Industry
	7 D Government Workers
	7 E Occupation and Residence in 1965
	7 F Occupations of Persons with High Earnings
Publication	Department of Commerce, Bureau of the Census Washington, DC: Government Printing Office
Date	7 C 1972; 7 A, B, D, E, F 1973

Classifications

Supt. of Documents	C 3.223/10:970/v.2/pts.7 A, B, C, D, E, F
Library of Congress	HA 201.1970.A568 v.2 pts.7 A, B, C, D, E, F
card	72-60036
Dewey	312.0973
University of Texas	1970.92 through 1970.97

Microforms

Research Pubns.	Film 1970 Reels 45 and 46
A.S.I.	ASI 1974 7 A 2533-37; 7 B 2533-23; 7 C 2533-3; 7 D 2533-31; 7 E 2533-22; 7 F 2533-35
Pages	7 A xix, 805, 21a; 7 B xiv, 376, 21a; 7 C xvi, 504, 12a; 7 D xvi, 241, 20a; 7 E xiv, 116, 21a; 7 F xiii, 119, 21a pages
Maps, illustrations	One map each in Parts 7 A and 7 E.
Notes	This is the basic group of reports on the subjects of occupation and industry. Demographic and socioeconomic data are provided in each report. The minimum income for "high earnings" in Part 7 F is $15,000.

1970
Volume II Subject Reports Parts 7 A, B, C, D, E and F

	A	B	C	D	E	F
Demographic Characteristics						
Aggregate population						
Limited to persons 14+ years		x				
Limited to persons 16+ years	x		x	x		x
Limited to persons 20-64 years					x	
Age	x	x			x	
Race	x	x	x	x	x	x
Spanish origin	x	x	x	x	x	x
Sex	x	x	x	x	x	x
Marital Status	x	x			x	
Social and Economic Characteristics						
Education						
Years of school completed	x	x	x	x	x	x
Employment	x	x	x	x	x	x
Weeks worked	x	x		x		x
Hours worked		x		x		
Class of employer	x	x		x		x
government employer				x		
last employer of unemployed			x			
Families	x			x		
Unpaid family workers	x					
Income	x	x		x	x	x
Industry	x	x	x		x	x
Labor force	x	x		x		x
Migration/mobility	x				x	
Military/veterans						
Armed forces 1965					x	

1970
Volume II   Subject Reports   Parts 7 A, B, C, D, E and F

	Part					
	A	**B**	**C**	**D**	**E**	**F**
Occupations	x	x	x	x	x	x
Wife/husband	x					x
Poverty		x				
Apportionment, Geography						
Regions	x	x		x	x	x
States				x		
Metropolitan/nonmetropolitan						x
Urban/rural	x	x				

Decennial Year	1970
Census	Nineteenth Decennial Census
Volume	Volume II Subject Reports Part 8
Titles	1970 Census of Population 8 A Sources and Structure of Family Income 8 B Earnings by Occupation and Education 8 C Income of the Farm-related Population
Publication	Department of Commerce, Bureau of the Census Washington, DC: Government Printing Office
Date	1973

Classifications

Supt. of Documents	C 3.223/10:970/v.2/pts.8 A, B, C
Library of Congress	HA 201.1970.A568 v.2 pts.8 A, B, C
card	72-60036
Dewey	312.0973
University of Texas	1970.98 through 1970.100

Microforms

Research Pubns.	Film 1970 Reels 46 and 47
A.S.I.	ASI 1974 8 A 2533-6; 8 B 2533-9; 8 C 2533-19
Pages	8 A xii, 475, 21a; 8 B x, 407, 21a; 8 C xi, 820, 24a pages
Maps, illustrations	One map in each part.
Notes	Each report in this group contains data on demographic characteristics as well as considerable social and economic data, with the most extensive data in Part 8 C on the farm-related population.

1970
Volume II Subject Reports Parts 8 A, B and C

	Part A	Part B	Part C
Demographic Characteristics			
Aggregate population	x		x
Persons 18-64 years		x	
Age	x	x	x
Race	x	x	x
Spanish origin	x	x	x
Sex	x	x	x
Marital status	x		x
Social and Economic Characteristics			
Education			
School enrollment			x
Years of school completed	x	x	x
Employment			x
Work experience		x	
Class employer			x
Families	x		x
Number earners	x		x
Farmers, farms			x
Households			x
Housing			x
Income	x		x
Earnings	x	x	x
Self-employment earnings	x		x
Wife/husband income	x		x
Unrelated individuals	x		x
Type income	x		x
Labor force	x	x	x

1970
Volume II   Subject Reports   Parts 8 A, B and C

	Part A	Part B	Part C
Occupations	x	x	x
Poverty	x		x
<u>Apportionment, Geography</u>			
Regions	x	x	
States			x
Metropolitan/nonmetropolitan	x		
Central cities	x		
Rural farm/nonfarm	x		x

Decennial Year	1970
Census	Nineteenth Decennial Census
Volume	Volume II Subject Reports Part 9
Titles	1970 Census of Population 9 A Low-Income Population 9 B Low-Income Areas in Large Cities
Publication	Department of Commerce, Bureau of the Census Washington, DC: Government Printing Office
Date	1973

Classifications

Supt. of Documents	C 3.223/10:970/v.2/pts.9 A, B
Library of Congress	HA 201.1970.A568 v.2 pts.9 A, B
card	72-60036
Dewey	312.0973
University of Texas	1970.101 and 1970.102

Microforms

Research Pubns.	Film 1970 Reels 47 and 48
A.S.I.	ASI 1974 9 A 2533-26; 9 B 2533-38
Pages	9 A xi, 465, 24a; 9 B xxxiv, 853, 24a pages
Maps, illustrations	9 A has one map.
Notes	Demographic and socioeconomic data are pro-vided in both parts. In Part 9 A it is given for regions and in Part 9 B, for 50 of the largest cities with 20 percent or higher poverty rates.

1970
Volume II Subject Reports Parts 9 A and B

	Part A	Part B
Demographic Characteristics		
Aggregate population		x
Residents of 50 largest cities with census tracts with poverty rates of 20+ percent		x
Age	x	x
Race	x	x
Spanish origin	x	x
Mexican, Puerto Rican, Cuban, Central or South American	x	
Sex	x	x
Marital status	x	x
Social and Economic Characteristics		
Disabilities	x	
Education		
School enrollment	x	x
Years of school completed	x	x
Persons 16-21, 16-24 not in school	x	x
Vocational training	x	
Employment/unemployment	x	x
Work experience	x	
Class employer	x	
Place of work re SMSA		x
Families	x	x
Fertility	x	x
Households		x
Housing	x	x

1970
Volume II Subject Reports Parts 9 A and B

	Part A	Part B
Income	X	X
Number family earners	X	
Unrelated individuals	X	X
Type income	X	X
Labor force	X	X
Migration/mobility	X	X
Military/veterans	X	X
Nativity		
Foreign stock		X
Country of origin	X	
Occupations		X
Poverty	X	X
Transportation		X

Apportionment, Geography

	Part A	Part B
Regions	X	
Metropolitan/nonmetropolitan	X	
Inside/outside central cities	X	
Size of place	X	
Urban/rural	X	
Cities - 50 largest		X
Census tracts		X
Low-income/non low-income areas		X

Decennial Year	1970
Census	Nineteenth Decennial Census
Volume	Volume II Subject Reports Part 10
Title	1970 Census of Population 10 A Americans Living Abroad 10 B State Economic Areas
Publication	Department of Commerce, Bureau of the Census Washington, DC: Government Printing Office
Date	10 A 1973; 10 B 1972
Classifications	
Supt. of Documents	C 3.223/10:970/v.2/pts.10 A, B
Library of Congress	HA 201.1970.A568 v.^ pts.10 A, B
card	72-60036
Dewey	312.0973
University of Texas	1970.103 and 1970.104
Microforms	
Research Pubns.	Film 1970 Reel 48
A.S.I.	ASI 1974 10 A 2533-30; 10 B 2533-2
Pages	10 A vii, 153, 19a; 10 B x, 425, 47a pages
Maps, illustrations	Part 10 B has 2 maps.
Notes	Separate questionnaires were used for Americans living abroad: one for armed forces personnel and one for civilians. Copies may be found in the appendix of Part 10 A. Demographic and socioeconomic data are provided for Americans living abroad and for persons counted by State Economic Areas.

1970
Volume II Subject Reports Parts 10 A and B

	Part A	Part B
Demographic Characteristics		
Aggregate population	x	
Age	x	x
Race	x	x
Spanish origin		x
Sex	x	
Marital status	x	
Social and Economic Characteristics		
Citizenship	x	
Education		
School enrollment	x	x
Years of school completed	x	x
Employment/unemployment	x	x
Class of employer	x	x
Families	x	x
Dependents of federal employees, armed forces		
members, civilian employees	x	
Fertility		x
Household		x
Group quarters		x
Income		x
Industry	x	x
Labor force	x	x

1970
Volume II Subject Reports Parts 10 A and B

	Part A	Part B
Language		
Ability to speak local language	x	
Mother tongue		x
Local employee/English speaker	x	
Migration/mobility	x	x
Country of residence	x	
Years since left the United States	x	
Nativity	x	x
General and parental nativity		x
Occupations	x	x
By country of home residence	x	
Crews of merchant vessels	x	
Poverty		x

Decennial Year   1970

Census   Nineteenth Decennial Census

Volume   Final Reports

Title   1970 Census of Population and Housing
                          Census Tracts Reports 1-241

Publication   Department of Commerce, Bureau of the Census
                          Washington, DC: Government Printing Office

Date   1971 and 1972

Classifications

  Supt. of Documents   C 3.223/11:970/1-241

  Library of Congress   HA 201.1970.A542 nos.1-241

    card   73-186611

  Dewey   312.0973

  University of Texas   1970.105 through 1970.349

Microforms

  Research Pubns.   Film 1970   Reels 49 through 70

Pages   Vary

Maps, illustrations   Maps of areas covered, census tracts and
                          usually an inset of tracts for central city.
                          Maps were either included in the printed re-
                          port or were printed on separate sheets to
                          accompany the report.

Notes   A <u>Census Tract</u> report was published for
                          each of the 241 Standard Metropolitan Statis-
                          tical Areas. They included 8 tables of data
                          from the 1970 Population Census and 5 tables
                          from the Housing Census. Certain tables in-
                          cluded data for the Negro population and for
                          the Spanish language population only.

                          These reports were designated PHC(1). For
                          areas which had been tracted by 1960, tables
                          showing comparability are included.

1970
Final Reports   Census Tracts

	SMSA	Component Parts	Tracts
Demographic Characteristics			
Aggregate population	Pl	Pl	Pl
Age	Pl,5	Pl,5	Pl,5
By sex	Pl,5	Pl,5	Pl,5
Race	Pl,5,6, H3,4	Pl,5,6, H3,4	Pl,5,6, H3,4
Spanish language	P2,7,8, H5	P2,7,8, H5	P2,7,8, H5
Sex	Pl,3, 5-8	Pl,3,5-8	Pl,3,5-8
Marital Status	Pl	Pl	Pl
Social and Economic Characteristics			
Education			
School enrollment	P2,5	P2,5	P2,5
persons not enrolled in school			
aged 16-21 years	P2,5	P2,5	P2,5
Years of school completed	P2,5	P2,5	P2,5
Employment	P3,6	P3,6	P3,6
Place of work in SMSA	P2	P2	P2
Class employer	P3	P3	P3
Families	Pl,5	Pl,5	Pl,5
Fertility	P2	P2	P2
Households	Pl,4,5	Pl,4,5	Pl,4,5
Housing	P4,Hl, 4,5	P4,Hl, 4,5	P4,Hl, 4,5
Income	P4,6	P4,6	P4,6
By type	P4	P4	P4

1970
Final Reports Census Tracts

	SMSA	Component Parts	Tracts
Industry	P3	P3	P3
Institutional population	P3	P3	P3
Labor force	P3,6	P3,6	P3,6
Language			
Spanish language, mother tongue	P2,7,8	P2,7,8	P2,7,8
Migration/mobility	P2,5,7	P2,5,7	P2,5,7
Nativity			
General nativity	P2	P2	P2
Foreign stock by country of			
origin	P2	P2	P2
Parentage	P2	P2	P2
Occupations	P3,6	P3,6	P3,6
Poverty	P4,6	P4,6	P4,6
Transportation	P2,H2	P2,H2	P2,H2

Decennial Year	1970
Census	Nineteenth Decennial Census
Volume	Final Reports
Title	1970 Census of Population and Housing General Demographic Trends for Metropolitan Areas, 1960 to 1970
Publication	Department of Commerce, Bureau of the Census Washington, DC: Government Printing Office
Date	1971

Classifications

Supt. of Documents	C 3.223/13:970/1-52
Library of Congress	HA 201.1970.A424
Dewey	312.0973
University of Texas	1970.350 through 1970.401

Microforms

Research Pubns.	Film 1970 Reel 71
A.S.I.	ASI 1974 2551-2.1 through 2551-2.52
Pages	Vary
Maps, illustrations	One map for each state showing the changes in its population between 1960 and 1970.
Notes	This is a series of 52 reports, one for the United States, one for each state, and one for the District of Columbia. Each report includes data from the population and housing censuses for the SMSAs and their constituent parts. An analytical text at the front of each report provides a valuable discussion of the possible explanation for population changes.
	These reports were designated PHC(2).

General Demographic Trends for Metropolitan Areas,
1960 to 1970

	State	SMSAs	Central Cities	Counties
Demographic Characteristics				
Aggregate population		1,2	3	2,3
Historic from 1960		1,2	3	2,3
Age	4	4	4	
Race	1,3,4	1,3,4	3	2
Percent	1	1		
Social and Economic Characteristics				
Housing	5			
Migration				
Net migration	3	3	3	3
Apportionment, Geography				
Inside/outside central cities	1,4,5	1,3,4	4	
Metropolitan areas	4,5			
Vital statistics				
Births	3	3	3	3
Deaths	3	3	3	3

Decennial Year	1970
Census	Nineteenth Decennial Census
Volume	Final Reports
Title	1970 Census of Population and Housing Employment Profiles of Selected Low-Income Areas
Publication	Department of Commerce, Bureau of the Census Washington, DC: Government Printing Office
Date	1971 and 1972
Classifications	
Supt. of Documents	C 3.223/17:970/1-76
Library of Congress	HD 5724.U581 1970
card	72-182144
Dewey	312.0973
University of Texas	1970.402 through 1970.477
Microforms	
Research Pubns.	Film 1970 Reels 72 through 80
A.S.I.	ASI 1974 2551-3.1 through 2551-3.76
Pages	Vary
Maps, illustrations	One map of the portion of each city showing the location of the employment survey area, and a map of the survey area on a larger scale.
Notes	These 76 reports with socioeconomic data for low-income areas (of 51 cities in 67 reports, 7 sets of rural counties in 8 reports, and a U.S. summary), unlike other 1970 census reports, resulted not from the enumeration of the population, but from a survey of predetermined areas. Copies of the survey questionnaire are included in the reports.
	The reports were designated PHC(3). Most tables have separate parts, a and b, which distinguish data for White and Negro population.

	Survey Area

Demographic Characteristics

Aggregate population
  Civilian noninstitutional population
    16+ years of age   A

Age
  Limited to persons 16+ years   A,1,6-9

Race   A-N, 1,2,4-11

Sex   A,C-N

Marital Status   A

Social and Economic Characteristics

Education
  School enrollment   C
  Educational attainment   C,M,1,3,4,44,45
  Job training   32-34

Employment/unemployment   D,F,G,H,M,
                                        3,6,19-23,28,29,35-38,49
  Unemployed   F,21,22

Families   A,B,1-3,7,40,41

Housing   L,43

Income, expenditures   H,I,L,7-10,24-27,30,31,
                                        42,47,48,51

Industry   8,10,11

Labor force   D,1
  Persons not in labor force   14-18

Migration/mobility   C,52-54

Military/veterans   C,M

1970
Final Reports   Employment Profiles of Selected Low-Income Areas

	Survey Area
Nativity	
In this city/elsewhere	C
Puerto Rico	C
Foreign born in Mexico, Cuba, other	C
Occupations	D,M
	4-6,8,11,33,37-39,50
Poverty	J,K
Transportation	N,11-13
Time for travel to work	N

NOTES ON OTHER 1970 CENSUS PUBLICATIONS
WITH POPULATION INFORMATION

VOLUME	TITLE

Supplementary Reports

There were 108 Supplementary Reports published as the result of the 1970 enumeration. Unlike 1960, some of the reports were special compilations not included in the final volumes. Other reports consisted of selected tables from longer reports in order to provide for less expensive publication. The series was numbered PC(S1) by the Census Bureau. The last report was published as late as 1979.

```
C 3.223/12:970/1-108
A.S.I.   ASI 1974 2535-1 through 55
         ASI 1975 2535 (includes some reports)
```

1. Distribution of the Negro Population. 8 pages. 1971.

2. Negro Population in Selected Places and Selected Counties. 17 pages. 1971.

3. 1970 Population of Voting Age for States. 11 pages. 1971.

4. Population of the United States, Puerto Rico, and Outlying Areas: 1950 to 1970. 2 pages. 1972.

5. Composition of the Urban Population: 1970. 3 pages. 1972.

6. Population and Land Area of Urbanized Areas: 1970 and 1960. 15 pages. 1972.

7. Population of Standard Metropolitan Statistical Areas: 1950 to 1970. 10 pages. 1972.

8. Population Annexed to Central Cities of Standard Metropolitan Statistical Areas in the United States between 1960 and 1970. 15 pages. 1972.

9. Population of Places of 10,000 or More by
    Wards. 20 pages. 1972.

10. Age of the Population of the United States:
    1970. 9 pages. 1972.

11. Race of the Population of the United States,
    by States: 1970. 3 pages. 1972.

12. Race and Urban and Rural Residence of the
    Population of the United States, by States:
    1970. 5 pages. 1972.

13. Age and Race of the Population of the United
    States, by States: 1970. 15 pages. 1972.

14. Household Relationship for Regions, Divi-
    sions, and States: 1970. 4 pages. 1972.

15. Race of the Population for Standard Metro-
    politian Statistical Areas, Urbanized
    Areas, and Places of 50,000 or More: 1970.
    12 pages. 1972.

16. Metropolitan and Nonmetropolitan Residence
    of the Population 65 Years Old and Over:
    1970. 3 pages. 1972.

17. Population of Standard Metropolitan Statis-
    tical Areas Established Since the 1970 Census
    for the United States: 1970 and 1960.
    8 pages. 1972.

18. Country of Origin of the Foreign Stock, for
    the United States: 1970 and 1960. 3 pages.
    1972.

19. Mobility, Commuting, and Veteran Status for
    the United States: 1970. 3 pages. 1972.

20. Educational Characteristics of the Popula-
    tion of the United States: 1970. 3 pages.
    1972.

21. Fertility and Family Composition for the
    United States: 1970. 4 pages. 1972.

22. Employment Status of the Population for the United States: 1970. 4 pages. 1972.

23. Occupation of Employed Persons for the United States: 1970. 4 pages. 1972.

24. Industry of Employed Persons for the United States: 1970. 4 pages. 1972.

25. Weeks Worked, Class of Workers, Last Occupation of the Experienced Unemployed, and Labor Mobility for the United States: 1970. 4 pages. 1972.

26. Population of Places of 2,500 or More: 1970 and 1960. 51 pages. 1972.

27. Rural Population by Farm-Nonfarm Residence for Counties in the United States: 1970. 27 pages. 1972.

28. Population of Congressional Districts for the 93rd Congress. 10 pages. 1972.

29. Population and Housing Characteristics for the United States, by States: 1970. 74 pages. 1972.

30. Persons of Spanish Ancestry. 24 pages. 1973.

31. Work Disability of Family Heads by Family Income in the United States: 1970. 6 pages. 1973.

32. Detailed Occupation of Employed Persons by Race and Sex for the United States: 1970. 9 pages. 1973.

33. Characteristics of Civilian Male Veterans for the United States: 1970. 4 pages. 1973.

34. Age at First Marriage and Children Ever Born for the United States: 1970. 10 pages. 1973.

35. Country of Origin, Mother Tongue, and Citizenship for the United States: 1970. 6 pages. 1973.

36. Educational Attainment by Age, Sex, and Race for the United States: 1970. 112 pages. 1973.

37. Detailed Industry of Employed Persons by Race and Sex for the United States: 1970. 7 pages. 1973.

38. Low-Income Families in 1969, by Type, Age, and Race of Head: 1970. 7 pages. 1973.

39. Age and Earnings by Occupation for the United States: 1970. 20 pages. 1973.

40. Marital Status and Living Arrangements of the Population in the United States: 1970. 13 pages. 1973.

41. Social and Economic Characteristics by Marital Status for the United States: 1970. 15 pages. 1973.

42. Selected Labor Force Characteristics of Persons and Families in the United States: 1970. 15 pages. 1973.

43. Family Income in 1969 by Family Characteristics for the United States: 1970. 19 pages. 1973.

44. Age and Earnings by Industry for the United States: 1970. 18 pages. 1973.

45. Patterns of Commuting in Large Metropolitan Areas: 1970. 4 pages. 1973.

46. Lifetime and Recent Migration by Educational Attainment for the United States: 1970. 9 pages. 1973.

47. Characteristics of Negro Immigrants to Selected Metropolitan Areas: 1970. 34 pages. 1973.

48. <u>Interstate Migration by State: 1970.</u> 20 pages. 1973.

49. <u>Social and Economic Characteristics by Detailed Industry for the United States: 1970.</u> 12 pages. 1973.

50. <u>Occupation and Residence in 1965, for the United States: 1970.</u> 11 pages. 1973.

51. <u>Fertility of Women by Education and Family Income for the United States: 1970.</u> 13 pages. 1973.

52. <u>Nativity and Parentage Composition of Families of Foreign Stock, for the United States: 1970.</u> 2 pages. 1973.

53. <u>Residence in 1965 for Selected Areas: 1970.</u> 69 pages. 1973.

54. <u>Household Income in 1969 for States, SMSA's, Cities and Counties: 1970.</u> 57 pages. 1973.

55. <u>Graphic Summary of the 1970 Population Census.</u> 54 pages. 1973.

56. <u>Selected Characteristics of the Population in Low-Income Areas of Large Cities: 1970.</u> 24 pages. 1973.

57. <u>Characteristics of the Spanish Surname Population by Census Tract, for SMSA's in Arizona: 1970.</u> 43 pages. 1974.

58. <u>Characteristics of the Spanish Surname Population by Census Tract, for SMSA's in California: 1970.</u> 614 pages. 1974.

59. <u>Characteristics of the Spanish Surname Population by Census Tract, for SMSA's in Colorado: 1970.</u> 54 pages. 1974.

60. <u>Characteristics of the Spanish Surname Population by Census Tract, for SMSA's in New Mexico: 1970.</u> 27 pages. 1974.

61. Characterisics of the Spanish Surname Population by Census Tract, for SMSA's in Texas: 1970. 229 pages. 1974.

62. Distribution of Foreign Stock Population: 1970. 17 pages. 1974.

63. Per Capita Income, Median Family Income, Low-Income Status in 1969 for States, Standard Metropolitan Statistical Areas, and Counties: 1970. 83 pages. 1974.

64. Native Population of Alaska by Race: 1970. 3 pages. 1974.

Low-Income Neighborhoods in Large Cities: 1970 (all 1974):

65. Atlanta, Georgia. 51 pages.

66. Baltimore, Maryland. 51 pages.

67. Birmingham, Alabama. 34 pages.

68. Boston, Massachusetts. 68 pages.

69. Buffalo and Rochester, New York. 34 pages.

70. Chicago, Illinois. 102 pages.

71. Cincinnati, Ohio. 34 pages.

72. Cleveland and Toledo, Ohio. 51 pages.

73. Columbus, Ohio. 34 pages.

74. Dallas and Fort Worth, Texas. 51 pages.

75. Denver, Colorado. 34 pages.

76. Detroit, Michigan. 85 pages.

77. El Paso, Texas. 34 pages.

78. Houston, Texas. 51 pages.

79. <u>Indianapolis, Indiana</u>. 17 pages.

80. <u>Jacksonville and Tampa, Florida</u>. 51 pages.

81. <u>Kansas City, Missouri</u>. 34 pages.

82. <u>Los Angeles, California</u>. 85 pages.

83. <u>Louisville, Kentucky</u>. 17 pages.

84. <u>Memphis and Nashville-Davison, Tennessee</u>.
    85 pages.

85. <u>Miami, Florida</u>. 34 pages.

86. <u>Milwaukee, Wisconsin</u>. 34 pages.

87. <u>Minneapolis and St. Paul, Minnesota</u>.
    34 pages.

88. <u>Newark, New Jersey</u>. 17 pages.

89. <u>New Orleans, Louisiana</u>. 51 pages.

90. <u>New York, New York</u>. 255 pages.

91. <u>Norfolk, Virginia</u>. 17 pages.

92. <u>Oklahoma City and Tulsa, Oklahoma</u>.
    34 pages.

93. <u>Omaha, Nebraska</u>. 34 pages.

94. <u>Philadelphia, Pennsylvania</u>. 68 pages.

95. <u>Phoenix, Arizona</u>. 17 pages.

96. <u>Pittsburgh, Pennsylvania</u>. 46 pages.

97. <u>Portland, Oregon</u>. 17 pages.

98. <u>St. Louis, Missouri</u>. 51 pages.

99. <u>San Antonio, Texas</u>. 51 pages.

100. <u>San Diego and San Jose, California</u>.
     34 pages.

---

101. <u>San Francisco and Oakland, California</u>.
     51 pages.

102. <u>Seattle, Washington</u>. 17 pages.

103. <u>Washingon, D.C.</u> 34 pages.

104. <u>Race of the Population by County: 1970</u>.
     70 pages. 1975.

105. <u>Poverty Status in 1969 and 1959 of Persons
     and Families, for States, SMSA's, Central
     Cities, and Counties: 1970 and 1960</u>.
     102 pages. 1975.

106. <u>Population of Urbanized Areas Established
     Since the 1970 Census for the United States:
     1970</u>. 59 pages. 1976.

107. <u>1970 Population of North Dakota by Township
     and City</u>. 18 pages. 1976.

108. <u>Population and Land Area of Urbanized Areas,
     for the United States: 1970 and 1960</u>. 354
     pages. 1979.

Indexes   <u>Alphabetical Index of Industries and Occupations</u>

1971
C 3.223:Oc1/970
HA 201.1970.A565   74-612012 MARC
331.0973
1970.478
Research Pubns. 1970 Reel 81
380 pages

This index, drawing on indexes from earlier decades, was developed for the purpose of classification of the occupations of those enumerated, and
the industries in which they were employed. The
lists are alphabetical, and contain 19,000 industries and 23,000 occupational titles.

Classified Index of Industries and Occupations

> 1971
> C 3.223:OC1/2/970
> HA 201.1970.A567   74-179488
> 338.00973
> 1970.479
> Research Pubns.   1970 Reel 81
> 265 pages
>
> This index, a companion to the one above, contains the same basic industries and occupations, but they are arranged by classification rather than alphabetically.

Guides

Census Users' Guide

> C3.2:6/2:C33/2/pts.1&2
> HA 37.U52 1970c   71-610123 MARC
> 001.4'22
>
> This heavily used guide is a major source of information about all aspects of the 1970 Census.

1970 Census of Population and Housing Procedural History

> C 3.223:P94/2/970
> HA 37.U52 1976   76-5793 MARC
> 312'.0973

1970 Census of Population and Housing: Data Collection Forms and Procedures

> C 3.223:F76/970
> HA 205.A5 1971   73-612497 MARC
> 001.4'33
> 115 pages

CENSUS GEOGRAPHIC AREAS

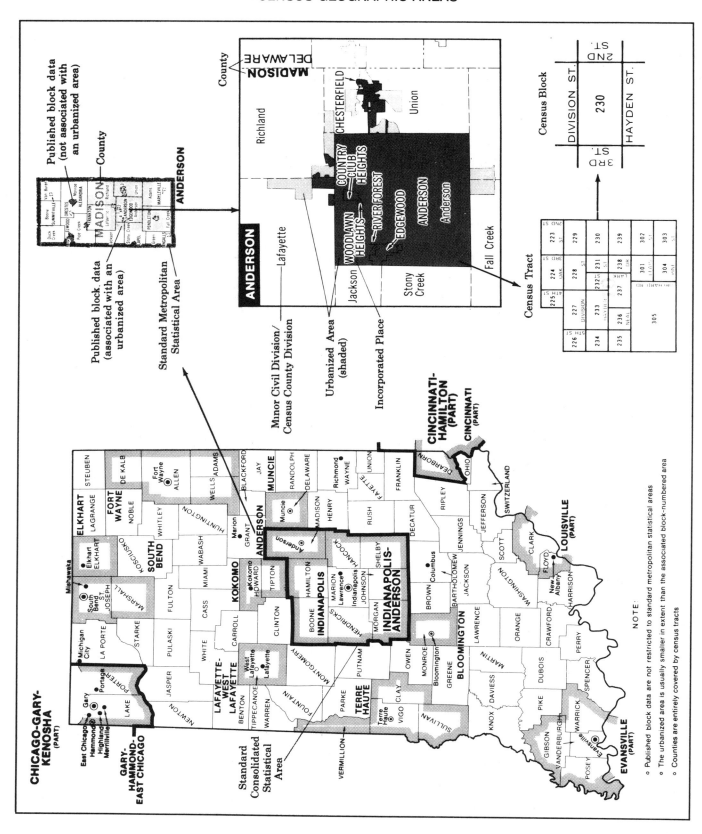

GEOGRAPHIC IDENTIFICATION CODE SCHEME

1980
POPULATION INFORMATION IN THE TWENTIETH DECENNIAL CENSUS

For the first time in over a century, no bound copies of reports resulting from the census were distributed by the federal government in 1980. Instead, a variety of population reports were published in paper covers with individual series printed in separate colors for easier organization and shelving. It is likely that many libraries had some or all of the 1980 census reports bound and that there is a great variety in their appearance in libraries throughout the country.

Population counts were distributed first as Preliminary Reports: Preliminary Population and Housing Unit Counts, in late 1980 and early 1981. They were followed by Advance Reports: Final Population and Housing Unit Counts. A separate report was published for each state, the District of Columbia, the outlying areas, and a summary for the United States. The latter includes data for regions, divisions, states and Congressional Districts. The Advance Reports superseded the Preliminary Reports. Each has but a few tables, and as is apparent from their titles, the count is restricted to total population and total housing units for each jurisdiction.

Following distribution of the above reports, the Census Bureau began to publish Volume I, Characteristics of the Population. Each chapter was published separately. Chapter A, Number of Inhabitants, came first, expanding on the data in the Advance Reports, with considerable information on urban and rural designation, land area and density, places of various sizes, and the population of Standard Metropolitan Areas and Standard Consolidated Statistical Areas.

Chapter B, General Population Characteristics, followed, with data from the "complete count" questions. These are the questions asked of the entire population: age, sex, race, marital status, relationship to the household, and, for the first time, Spanish origin. The latter question had been asked only of a sample portion of the population in prior decades.

Chapter C, General Social and Economic Characteristics, and Chapter D, Detailed Population Characteristics, contain information gleaned from the sample questions, cross-classified by age, sex, race, marital status, household relationship and Spanish origin. Chapter C of the United States Summary carries data down to the level of urbanized areas and places, but Chapter D is restricted to data for Regions and Standard Consolidated Statistical Areas. Likewise, the state Chapter C's carry information down to the smallest places, but their Chapter D's contain detailed data only for the state as a whole and for Standard Metropolitan Statistical Areas with populations of 250,000 or more.

1980
Introduction

The four chapters of Volume I were followed by thirteen <u>Subject Reports</u>. An even larger number of such publications had been proposed and even named and numbered, but apparently insufficient funding prevented their being published. The subjects of most of these reports had been included in similar publications in earlier censuses. The introductory pages provide references to the exact titles for former years. The <u>Subject Reports</u> were designated Volume II.

Twenty <u>Supplementary Reports</u> were published for 1980, in contrast to the hundred-plus for 1970. These reports are very useful publications and contain valuable introductory essays on their specific subjects. One, new in 1980, was that titled <u>Ancestry of the Population by State</u>.

The reports already discussed were those with data from the Census of Population alone. The reports to follow contain data from both the Census of Population and the Census of Housing.

A very useful addition of the 1980 Census was a set of <u>Summary Characteristics for Governmental Units and Standard Metropolitan Statistical Areas</u> published for each state, the District of Columbia and for Puerto Rico. These reports contain social and economic characteristics as well as housing data for Standard Metropolitan Statistical Areas, counties, and all incorporated places, no matter how small. Because of their simplicity, these reports are often the best place to start looking for 1980 census data.

The <u>Advance Estimates of Social, Economic and Housing Characteristics</u> are another new set of reports, one for each state, with data for counties and for cities of 25,000. They are succinct and also very easy to use.

A third group, also published for each state, is <u>Congressional Districts of the 98th Congress</u>. Reports for the 99th and a few for the 100th Congress were published for those states which redistricted later. These reports provide both complete and sample data for the fifty states and the District of Columbia.

A large set of reports made up the 380 <u>Census Tract</u> publications. These are accompanied by a set of maps showing tract boundaries.

374 <u>Block Statistics</u> reports for Standard Metropolitan Statistical Areas were issued in microfiche, accompanied by printed maps.

1980
Introduction

A number of other 1980 reports were published only in microform. They are not included in this guide, as it is limited to printed volumes. Those needing the more precise information of the various files published on microfiche should consult the catalogs published by the Census Bureau.

Population Inquiries

The 1980 census continued the system begun in 1960 and used again in 1970 of making inquiries of the entire population only as to basic demographic data: age, sex, race, marital status, and relationship to the household. However, the term "head of household" was dropped and "household relationship" took its place. For the first time, Spanish origin was included as a demographic factor. Neither the Census Bureau nor census users had been satisfied with data on the Spanish origin population in 1960, when efforts were first made to count it, nor in 1970, when a more extensive effort had been made.

Sample items in 1980 included those on citizenship, disabilities (but only asked of those of working age), education, employment, immigration, income, industry, language, migration, nativity and ancestry, occupation, residence in 1975, veteran status and travel to work.

Sample questions were asked of at least every sixth household, furnishing a 17 percent sample. In places, counties and minor civil divisions of less than 2,500 population, sample questions were asked in every other household, thus furnishing a 50 percent sample.

1980
MAJOR POPULATION VOLUMES OF THE TWENTIETH DECENNIAL CENSUS

VOLUME	TITLE

Volume I   Characteristics of the Population

            Chapter A   Number of Inhabitants
              Part 1   United States Summary
              Parts 2-58   States and Outlying Areas

            Chapter B   General Population Characteristics
              Part 1   United States Summary
              Parts 2-58   States and Outlying Areas

            Chapter C   General Social and Economic Characteristics
              Part 1   United States Summary
              Parts 2-58   States and Outlying Areas

            Chapter D   Detailed Population Characteristics
              Part 1   United States Summary
              Parts 2-55   States and Outlying Areas

Volume II   Subject Reports

            1 D   American Indians, Eskimos, and Aleuts on Identified Reservations and in the Historic Areas of Oklahoma. Parts 1 and 2
            1 E   Asian and Pacific Islander Population in the United States: 1980

            2 A   Geographical Mobility for States and the Nation
            2 C   Geographical Mobility for Metropolitan Areas

            4 B   Living Arrangements of Children and Adults
            4 C   Marital Characteristics
            4 D   Persons in Institutions and Other Group Quarters

            6 C   Journey to Work: Metropolitan Commuting Flows
            6 D   Journey to Work: Characteristics of Workers in Metropolitan Areas
            6 E   Place of Work

            7 C   Occupation by Industry

            8 B   Earnings by Occupation and Education
            8 D   Poverty Areas in Large Cities and Addendum

1980
Major Population Volumes

VOLUME		TITLE
Volume II (continued)	9 C	Characteristics of the Rural and Farm-Related Population
Supplementary Reports	S-1	Age, Sex, Race, and Spanish Origin of the Population by Regions, Divisions, and States: 1980
	S-2	Population and Households by States and Counties: 1980
	S-3	Race of the Population by States: 1980
	S-4	Population and Households for Census Designated Places: 1980
	S-5	Standard Metropolitan Statistical Areas and Standard Consolidated Statistical Areas: 1980
	S-6	Nonpermanent Residents by States and Selected Counties and Incorporated Places: 1980
	S-7	Persons of Spanish Origin by State: 1980
	S-8	Detailed Occupation and Years of School Completed by Age, for the Civilian Labor Force by Sex, Race, and Spanish Origin: 1980
	S-9	State of Residence in 1975 by State of Residence in 1980
	S-10	Ancestry of the Population by State: 1980
	S-11	Congressional District Profiles, 98th Congress
	S-12	Asian and Pacific Islander Population by State: 1980
	S-13	American Indian Areas and Alaska Native Villages: 1980
	S-14	Population and Land Area of Urbanized Areas for the United States and Puerto Rico: 1980 and 1970

**1980
Major Population Volumes**

VOLUME	TITLE
Supplementary Reports (continued)	S-15 Detailed Occupation of the Experienced Civilian Labor Force by Sex for the United States and Regions: 1980 and 1970
	S-16 Residence in 1975 for States by Age, Sex, Race, and Spanish Origin
	S-17 Gross Migration for Counties: 1975 to 1980
	S-18 Metropolitan Statistical Areas (as Defined by the Office of Management and Budget in 1983)
	S-19 Rural and Farm Population by Current (1980) and Previous (1970) Farm Definitions, for States and Counties: 1980
	S-20 Selected Characteristics of Persons with a Work Disability by State: 1980
Advance Reports	Advance Reports: Final Population and Housing Unit Counts
Final Reports	1980 Census of Population and Housing Census Tracts
	1980 Census of Population and Housing Summary Characteristics for Governmental Units and Standard Metropolitan Statistical Areas
	1980 Census of Population and Housing Congressional Districts of the 98th, 99th and 100th Congresses

Notes on other publications of the 1980 Census that contain population information are provided at the end of the 1980 section.

Decennial Year   1980

Census   Twentieth Decennial Census

Volume   Volume I Chapter A Part 1

Title   1980 Census of Population
                              Characteristics of the Population
                              Number of Inhabitants
                              United States Summary

Publication   Department of Commerce, Bureau of the Census
                              Washington, DC: Government Printing Office

Date   1983

Classifications

Supt. of Documents   C 3.223/5:980/v.1/A 1

Library of Congress   HA 201.1980.A13 v.1 ch.A pt.1

  card   81-607950

Dewey   312.0973

Census designation   PC80-1-A1

Microforms

A.S.I.   ASI 1983 2531-1.1

Pages   269, 15 app. pages

Maps, illustrations   None

Notes   Chapter A contains final population counts
                              in 36 tables, for each Census Region, Division,
                              state, Standard Metropolitan Statistical Area,
                              county, urbanized area and place of 2,500
                              population in the United States.

1980
Volume I   Characteristics of the Population   Chapter A   Number of Inhabitants   Part 1   United States Summary

	United States	Regions, Division, States, Counties	SCSAs, SMSAs, Ur.Areas, Places
Demographic Characteristics			
Aggregate Population	1-3, 8-10		
Historic from 1790	2,3,8-10		
percent change	9		
percent distribution	10		
Outlying areas	1		
Population abroad	1		
Regions, Divisions, States		8	
historic from 1790		8	
decennial rates of change		9	
percent distribution		10	
Urbanized areas			34
by rank			35
Counties		17	
by rank		18	
Places of 2,500			25
historic from 1960			25
Towns, townships			26
historic from 1960			26
Cities of 100,000			27
historic from 1790			27
50 largest, from 1850			28
Standard Consolidated Statistical Areas			29
historic from 1960			29
component parts			29
Standard Metropolitan Statistical Areas			30
historic from 1960			30
component parts			30
by rank			31
by definitions at earlier censuses			33
Urbanized areas			34
by rank			35
Tracted areas			36

1980
Volume I   Characteristics of the Population   Chapter A   Number of
Inhabitants   Part 1   United States Summary

	United States	Regions, Divisions, States, Counties	SCSAs, SMSAs, Ur.Areas, Places
Apportionment, Geography			
Apportionment	A,12	A,12	
Historic from 1790	B,12	B,12	
Density	1,2,11	11	
Rank by density		16	
States and counties		17	
Places of 2,500			25
Standard Metropolitan Statistical			
Areas			30
Urbanized areas			34
Size of place	4,5,14	14	
Historic from 1970	4		
Counties		19	
Inside/outside SMSAs	6,7,15	15	36
Urban/rural	3-6,13	13,16	
Historic from earliest census	5	13	
Urban inside/outside urbanized			
areas	15	15	
Number counties			
By population size	19	19	
By land area	20	20	
By percent urban	21	21	
By percent population change	22	22	
By number and type subdivisions	23	23	
Number and types of places,			
incorporated places, census-			
designated places	24	24	
Number census tracts in tracted			
areas	36	36	

Decennial Year	1980
Census	Twentieth Decennial Census
Volume	Volume I Chapter A Parts 2-58
Title	1980 Census of Population Characteristics of the Population Number of Inhabitants States and Outlying Areas
Publication	Department of Commerce, Bureau of the Census Washington, DC: Government Printing Office
Date	1981, 1982, 1983

Classifications

Supt. of Documents	C 3.223/5:980/v.1/A 2-58
Library of Congress	HA 201.1980.A13 v.1 ch.A pts.2-58
card	81-607950
Dewey	312.0973
Census designation	PC80-1-A-2-58

Microforms

A.S.I.	ASI 1981, 1982, 1983 2531-1.2 through 2531-1.58

Pages	Vary
Maps, illustrations	Maps of the state, SMSAs, counties, Census County Divisions, places and urbanized areas as well as several charts.
Notes	Parts 2 through 52 are state reports plus the District of Columbia. Part 53 is Puerto Rico. Parts 54-57 are combined in one volume and include Guam, the U.S. Virgin Islands, American Samoa, the Northern Marianas and the Trust Territory of the Pacific Islands.
	This chapter has 13 tables. They contain all the final population counts for the state, SMSAs, counties, county subdivisions, urbanized areas and places.

1980
Volume I Characteristics of the Population Chapter A Number of
Inhabitants Parts 2-58 States and Outlying Areas

	State	SMSAs	Counties, Subdvns.	Places
Demographic Characteristics				
Aggregate population	1,2,4	11,12	4	4-6
Historic from earliest census	1			
from 1930	2		2	
from 1960	4	11	4	4,5,11
from 1970				6
Rank				6
Urbanized areas				13
Apportionment, Geography				
Density	2		2	
Size of places	1,7-10	9		
Historic from 1930	8			
Urban/rural	1,3,7-9	12	3	
Historic from 1930	8			
from 1970			3	
Inside/outside urbanized areas	3,7		3	
Inside/outside SMSAs	9,10	12		
Inside/outside census-designated				

Decennial Year	1980
Census	Twentieth Decennial Census
Volume	Volume I Chapter B Part 1
Title	1980 Census of Population Characteristics of the Population General Population Characteristics United States Summary
Publication	Department of Commerce, Bureau of the Census Washington, DC: Government Printing Office
Date	1983

Classifications

Supt. of Documents	C 3.223/6:980/v.1/B 1
Library of Congress	HA 201.1980.A13 v.1 ch.B pt.1
card	81-607950
Dewey	312.0973
Census designation	PC80-1-B1

Microforms

A.S.I.	ASI 1983 2531-2.1

Pages	v, 334, 23a pages
Maps, illustrations	18 colored maps and charts.
Notes	The U.S. Summary, Part B, includes Tables 37-71. Data are provided not only for the United States, but for Regions, Divisions, states, Standard Consolidated Statistical Areas, Standard Metropolitan Statistical Areas, urbanized areas, places of 50,000, towns and townships of 50,000, Indian reservations and Alaska Native villages.

1980
**Volume I Characteristics of the Population Chapter B General
Population Characteristics Part 1 United States Summary**

	United States	Regs., Divns.	States	Other
Demographic Characteristics				
Aggregate population	37,61	61	61,67	68,68a, 70
Age	41-45, 47-49	54-61	61,67	68,68a, 71
Median	37,64	61,64	61,64	68,68a, 71
Single years by race, sex and Spanish origin	41			
historic from 1880	42			
By race and sex	44	58	67	
historic from 1910	45			
By race, sex and Spanish origin	41	53		
Race	37,62-66	50,52, 61-66	61-66	68,68a, 71
By sex	38,62	50,62	62,67	69,70
historic from 1900	40			
By age	43,37	58		
American Indians on reservations				71
Spanish origin	37,49, 63-66	51,60, 61,63-66	61,63-67	68,68a
By sex	64	64	64	
by age	41,42	59,60,63	63	
by race	39	51		
By type: Mexican, Puerto Rican, Cuban, other	48	51,59	63	70
Sex	43,61	54,61	61	69,71
Nearly all tables are by sex				
Marital status	37,46-49, 65	56,61,65	61,65	
Social and Economic Characteristics				
Families	46,49,66	56,66	66	71

1980
Volume I Characteristics of the Population Chapter B General
Population Characteristics Part 1 United States Summary

	United States	Regs., Divns.	States	Other
Fertility	37,61	61	61	68
Households	37,46-49	56,59-61	61,66	68,71
By age, race and Spanish origin	46	56		
Group quarters	37,46-49	56,59-61	61	68
Institutional population	46-49	56,59, 60		

Apportionment, Geography

Size of place	37			
Urban/rural	37			
Age	41,43	64	64	
Race by sex	38	50,54, 56,62	62,64	
Spanish origin	39,43	51,54, 62,63	62,63	
Marital status	56,65			
Families	46	56		
Households	46	56		
Indian reservations				71
Alaska Native villages				71

Decennial Year	1980
Census	Twentieth Decennial Census
Volume	Volume I Chapter B Parts 2-58
Title	1980 Census of Population Characteristics of the Population General Population Characteristics States and Outlying Areas
Publication	Department of Commerce, Bureau of the Census Washington, DC: Government Printing Office
Date	1982, 1983

Classifications

Supt. of Documents	C 3.223/6:980/v.1/B 2-58
Library of Congress	HA 201.1980.A13 v.1 ch.B pts.2-58
card	81-607950
Dewey	312.0973
Census designation	PC80-1-B-2-58

Microforms

A.S.I.	ASI 1982, 1983 2531-2.2 through 2531-2.58
Pages	Vary
Maps, illustrations	Map of Standard Metropolitan Statistical Areas, counties and selected places, county subdivisions, places and Indian reservations.
Notes	The Appendix contains a copy of the 1980 10^n percent questions for both population and housing, as well as definitions of all terms used for the data in this volume. This chapter has Tables 14-55. They contain the basic demographic, social and economic characteristics data for the state.

1980
Volume I Characteristics of the Population Chapter B General
Population Characteristics Parts 2-58 States and Outlying Areas

	State	SCSAs, SMSAs	Counties, Subdvns.	Places
Demographic Characteristics				
Aggregate population	14,16	14,16	14-16,44	14,16, 32-34
Indian reservations				55
Age	14,21	14,25	14,44-46, 50-52,54	14,25, 32,38, 39,41, 42,54
Single years, by race and sex and by Spanish origin	18			
Historic from 1910	20			
from 1970		26		26,33
Race	14-16, 21,22	14-16, 25,27, 30	14-16, 44,45, 47-51,53, 54	14-16, 25,27, 30-32, 34-36, 41,42, 54
White, Black, American Indian, Eskimo, Aleut, Japanese, Chinese, Filipino, Korean, Asian Indian, Vietnamese, Hawaiian, Guamanian, Samoan, other	15,22	15	15	15
Historic from 1900, by sex	17			
By age	18,22	25		25
Spanish origin	14,16, 23,24	14,16, 25,27, 29,31	14,16, 44,47-49, 51,54	14,16, 25,27, 29,31, 32,34- 36,38, 39,41, 54
By area of origin	16,23	16	16,53	16
By age	18,24	25	46	25
By sex	18,19, 23,24		45	

1980
Volume I Characteristics of the Population Chapter B General
Population Characteristics Parts 2-58 States and Outlying Areas

	State	SCSAs, SMSAs	Counties, Subdvns.	Places
Sex	17,18	30-32	50-54	30-32, 38,54
Marital status	14,21-24	14,28-31	14,49, 52	14,28-30,31, 36,38

Social and Economic Characteristics

	State	SCSAs, SMSAs	Counties, Subdvns.	Places
Families	21-24	27-31	47-51	27-31, 34-41
By race	22,24			
By Spanish origin	23			
Fertility	14	14	14	14
Households	14, 21-24, 28-54	14,27-31	14,44,47, 48,50-53	14, 27-31, 34-41, 43
Group quarters	14, 21-24	14,27, 28,30-31	14,47, 48,50-53	14,27, 28,30, 31,34, 35,37-41
Institutional population	21-24	27,28, 31	47,48, 50-53	27,28, 30,31, 34,35, 38-41

Apportionment, Geography

	State	SCSAs, SMSAs	Counties, Subdvns.	Places
Inside/outside SMSAs	14-17,19	25-31		25-31
Inside/outside urbanized areas	14-17,19			

1980
Volume I   Characteristics of the Population   Chapter B   General
Population Characteristics   Parts 2-58   States and Outlying Areas

	State	SCSAs, SMSAs	Counties, Subdvns.	Places
Size of place	14-16, 19,21			
Urban/rural	14-17,19, 21			
Age	19			
Race	14,19,21			
Spanish origin	14,19,21			
Sex	19			
Marital status	21			
Families	21			
Households	21			

Decennial Year	1980
Census	Twentieth Decennial Census
Volume	Volume I Chapter C Part 1
Title	1980 Census of Population Characteristics of the Population General Social and Economic Characteristics United States Summary
Publication	Department of Commerce, Bureau of the Census Washington, DC: Government Printing Office
Date	1983

Classifications

Supt. of Documents	C 3.223/7:980/v.1/C 1
Library of Congress	HA 201.1980.A13 v.1 ch.C pt.1
card	81-607950
Dewey	312.0973
Census designation	PC80-1-C-1

Microforms

A.S.I.	ASI 1984 2531-3.1
Pages	vii, 504, 60 app. pages
Maps, illustrations	34 maps and charts
Notes	This chapter includes Tables 72-252, which provide the major social and economic characteristics data for the United States, classified by the demographic characteristics of age, sex, marital status, race and Spanish origin.

192

1980
Volume I Characteristics of the Population Chapter C General
Social and Economic Characteristics Part 1 United States Summary

	United States	Regions, Divisions, States	SCSAs, SMSAs, Ur.Areas, Places
Demographic Characteristics			
Aggregate population	72	182,230	246
Age	98,109,120,130, 140,150,160, 166,172	204,235	251
Persons 60+ years	98,109,120,130, 140,172	182,193, 230,235	246
Race	74,120-129,140- 149	204-210	248,248a
Detailed race	160-165		248,248a
White	210-213		
Black	214-217		
American Indian, Eskimo, Aleut on reservations and Alaska Native villages	218-221		251,252
Asian and Pacific Islanders	222-225		
Spanish origin	75,130,139, 150-159	204-210, 226,229, 233	249,249a
By race and sex	75,130		
By origin	166-171		
Sex	74	182	
Marital status	100,103,111, 121,131,141, 151,173,176	184,187, 195,198, 237,240	
Social and Economic Characteristics			
Citizenship	77,79,99	183,236	
Disabilities	106,117,127,137, 147,157,161,167	190,201, 205,211	

1980
Volume I Characteristics of the Population Chapter C General Social and Economic Characteristics Part 1 United States Summary

	United States	Regions, Divisions, States	SCSAs, SMSAs, Ur.Areas, Places
Education			
School enrollment and years of school completed, identical tables	72,81,82,102, 113,123,133,143, 153,160,166,175	186,197, 204,210, 214,218, 222,226, 230,239, 246	251
School enrollment, from 1910	81		
School completed, from 1940	83		
Employment	89,127,137,147, 176	188,189, 198-200, 207,241, 242	252
Historic from 1970	89		
Weeks worked	88,106,127,137, 147,157,179	88	
Class of employer	90,91,103,114, 124,134,144,154, 162,168,176	184,187, 198,206, 212,216, 220,224, 225,240	
Families	72,100,111,121, 131,141,151, 161,167,173, 179	184,195, 205,210, 214,218, 222,226, 230,231, 237	246,247, 251,252
Fertility	72,84,100,111, 121,131,141,151, 160,166,173	184,195, 204,210, 214,218, 222,226, 230,237	246,251
Households	72,98,100,111, 120,121,130,131, 141,151,160,166, 172,173	182,184, 193,195, 204,235, 237	246,252

194

1980
Volume I Characteristics of the Population   Chapter C General
Social and Economic Characteristics   Part 1 United States Summary

	United States	Regions, Divisions, States	SCSAs, SMSAs, Ur.Areas, Places
Immigration	99,110	183,194, 236	
Income	73,92-95,107, 118,128,138,148, 158,164,170,180	191,192, 202,203, 208,213, 217,221, 225,229, 231,244	247,252
Industry	90,105,116,126, 136,146,156, 162,168,178	189,200, 206,211, 215,219, 223,227, 231,242	
Institutional population	101,120,121,130, 131,140,141		
Labor force	73,86,87,103, 106,111,114,117, 124,127,134,144, 154,162,168,176, 179	87,184, 190,198, 201,206, 215,219, 223,227	
Status of family members	100,106,121,131, 141,151,173		
Persons 16-19 years, by school enrollment	102,113,123,133, 143,153,175	186	
Language	99	183	
Language spoken at home	72,110	183,194, 230,236	251
Ability to speak English	110	183,194, 230,236	
Migration/mobility	72,78,80,101, 112,122,132,142, 152,161,167, 174	185,196, 210,214, 218,222, 230,238	246

SCSAs, United States	Regions, Divisions, States	SMSAs, Ur.Areas, Places
Military/veterans	85,101,111,112, 122,127,132,137, 147,157,161,167, 179	190,196	
Veterans by period of service	85,106,127,137, 147	185,201, 205,238, 241	
Nativity	72,77,79,101,122, 132		246,250, 250a
General nativity	99,142,152,161, 167,174	183,185, 194,196, 205,210, 214,218, 222,226, 238	
Specific by country of birth	79,99,110	79	
Ancestry	76,172-181	234	250,250a
Occupations	89,104,113, 115,125,135,145, 155,163,169, 177	188,199, 207,212, 216,220, 224,228, 241	
Poverty	73,96,97,108, 119,129,139, 149,159,165, 171,181	192,203, 209,213, 217,221, 225,229, 231,245	
Transportation			247
Travel time to work	101,122,132,142,	196,238	
Means of travel to work	101,112,122,132, 142,161,167,174	185,196, 205,210, 214,218, 222,226, 238	

196

1980
Volume I Characteristics of the Population Chapter C General
Social and Economic Characteristics Part 1 United States Summary

	United States	Regions, Divisions, States	SCSAs, SMSAs, Ur.Areas, Places
Transportation (continued)			
Disability, unable to use public transportation	127,137,161,167	190,243	
Apportionment, Geography			
Inside/outside SMSAs	109-119	193-203	
By race	140-149		
By Spanish origin	150-159		
Urban/rural	77	77,182	
Age	120,130,140, 150		
Race	74,120-129, 140-149		
Spanish origin	130-139, 150-159		
Sex	74		
Education	123,133	186	
Employment	124,134		
Families	121		
Fertility	121,131,141	184	
Households	120,130,140, 150		
Income	128	191	
Industry	122,136	189	
Labor force	124	187,190	
Migration/mobility	122,132	185	
Military/veterans	127	183	
Nativity	122,132		
Occupations	125,135	188	
Poverty	129	192	
Transportation	122,132		

Decennial Year	1980
Census	Twentieth Decennial Census
Volume	Volume I Chapter C Parts 2-58
Title	1980 Census of Population Characteristics of the Population General Social and Economic Characteristics States and Outlying Areas
Publication	Department of Commerce, Bureau of the Census Washington, DC: Government Printing Office
Date	1983, 1984
Classifications	
Supt. of Documents	C 3.223/7:980/v.1/C 2-58
Library of Congress	HA 201.1980.A13 v.1 ch.C pts.2-58
card	81-607950
Dewey	312.0973
Census designation	PC80-1-C2-58
Microforms	
A.S.I.	ASI 1983,1984 2531-3.2 through 2531-3.58
Pages	Vary
Maps, illustrations	One map in each part.
Notes	This chapter includes Tables 56-191. These tables provide the major social and economic characteristics data for the states and out-lying areas, classified by the demographic characteristics of age, sex, marital status, race and Spanish origin.

1980
Volume I Characteristics of the Population Chapter C General
Social and Economic Characteristics Parts 2-58 States and
Outlying Areas

	State	SCSAs, SMSAs	Counties	Places
Demographic Characteristics				
Aggregate population	56	56	56,177	56
Rural portion of counties			188	
Indian reservations				192,193
Age	62		171,188	
By race	58,73	126,132, 138,144	182	126,132 138,144
By Spanish origin	93,99	150	182	150
Persons 60+ years	73,83	115	171	115
By sex	62	115	171	115
Race	58,73, 76,77	58	58,188, 190	58,192
By age	73			
By sex	58	58	58	58
Spanish origin	59,83- 92,99-104	59,150	59,188	59,150
By race and sex	59			
By country of origin	59			
Sex	58	58	58,188, 190	58
Marital status	67,77,87	120		120,158
Marital history	64,74,84	117	173,176	117
Social and Economic Characteristics				
Citizenship	63	116		116
Disabilities - from ability				
to work and use public transit	70,112	123	179	123,157, 163
By race	80,94	127,133, 139,145	183	127,133, 139,145
By Spanish origin	90,100	151	183	151

1980
Volume I Characteristics of the Population Chapter C General Social and Economic Characteristics Parts 2-58 States and Outlying Areas

	State	SCSAs, SMSAs	Counties	Places
Education				
School enrollment	56,61,66	11,56, 119	56,175	56,119, 157,166
historic from 1900	6			
by race	76,93	126,132, 138,144	182	126,132, 138,144
by Spanish origin	86,99	150		150,162
by type of school	66	119		119
by labor force status	66	119		119
Years of school completed	56,61, 66	56,119	56,175, 188,190	119,157, 166
by race	76,93	126,132, 138,144	182	126,132, 138,144
by Spanish origin	86,99	150	182	150,162
Persons 16-19 years not in school and not high school graduates				192
Employment/unemployment	61			193
Place of work	57,65,75, 85,94,100			
Class of employer	67,77,87, 101			
Families	56	117	173	117,166
By race	74,94	127,133, 139,145	183	127,133, 137,145, 157
By Spanish origin	84,100	151	183	151,162, 169
Type of family	64			
By labor force status	64			
Number workers in family	57,70, 80,90	123,130, 136,142, 148	179,186	123,130, 136,142, 148,154, 158
Fertility	56,64	56	56,188, 190	56
By race	74,93, 99	126,133, 138,144	182	126,133, 138,144
By Spanish origin	84,99	150	182	150,162

1980
Volume I Characteristics of the Population Chapter C General Social and Economic Characteristics Parts 2-58 States and Outlying Areas

	State	SCSAs, SMSAs	Counties	Places
Households	56	56,117	56,171	56,117
By age – persons 60+ years	62	115	173	115
in group quarters	62	115	171	115
By race	74,93	126,132, 138,144	182	126,132, 138,144
By Spanish origin	84,99	150	182	150
Persons per household	62,73,83	117	171	117
Group quarters	62,73,83	117	17,173	117
Immigration	63	116	172	116
Income	57,71	57,124, 125	57,180, 189,191	57,124, 160,168
By race	81	130,136, 142,148	186	130,136, 142,148
By Spanish origin	91	154	186	154,165, 170
Industry	57,67, 79,89	57,122	57,178, 188,190	57,122, 167
By race	79	128,134, 140,146, 152	184	128,134, 140,146, 152
By Spanish origin	101	154	184	154,163
Institutional population	99	117	173	117
By type institution	64,74,84			
Labor force	57,61, 66,67,70	120,123	173,176, 179,189	120,123, 158
Historic from 1970	61			
By race	74,77,80	128,134, 140,146	184	128,132, 140,146
By Spanish origin	96,97, 101,103	152	184	152,163, 169
Family members in labor force		117		117
Language	56	56,116	56,172	56,116, 166
Spoken at home	63	116	172	116
Ability to speak English	63	116	172	116

1980
Volume I Characteristics of the Population Chapter C General
Social and Economic Characteristics Parts 2-58 States and
Outlying Areas

	State	SCSAs, SMSAs	Counties	Places
Migration/mobility	56,65	56,118	56,188, 190	56,118, 156
By race	75,94			
By Spanish origin	85,100			
Residence in 1975	61,65			
Military/veterans	80,90,94			
Veteran status	70			
Period of service	70			
By race	75,80			
Nativity				
General nativity	56	56	56	56
by race	75,94			
By Spanish origin	85,100			
Foreign born by country of				
birth	61			
historic from 1970	61			
Ancestry	60,105	60	60	60
by age and sex	105			
by marital status	105,109			
by disability	112			
by education	108			
by employment	106			
by family status	106			
by households	105,106			
by income	113			
by industry	111			
by labor force status	109,112			
by migration/mobility	107			
by nativity	107			
by poverty level	114			
by transportation	112			
Occupations	68			
By race	78,96			
By Spanish origin	92,98			
Poverty	57,72			
By race	82			
By Spanish origin	92,98			

1980
**Volume I Characteristics of the Population Chapter C General
Social and Economic Characteristics Parts 2-58 States and
Outlying Areas**

	State	SCSAs, SMSAs	Counties	Places
Transportation	57,75,85, 94,199			
To work	65			
by race	75,94			
travel time	65,75,85			
Apportionment, Geography				
Inside/outside SMSA's	58			
Sizes of places	58			
Urban/rural	62			
By age	62,73			
persons 60+ years	62,83			
By race	58,73			
By Spanish origin	59,83			
By sex	58			
By marital status, history	74,84			
Citizenship	63			
Disabilities	80,90			
Education	66,76,86			
Employment	65,77,80, 87,90			
Families	64,74,84			
Fertility	64,74,84			
Households	64,73,74,83,84			
Income	71,72,81,91			
Industry	60,64,79,89			
Labor force	64,67,70, 76,77,84, 86,87			
Language	63			
Migration/mobility	60,64,75,85			
Military/veterans	80,90			
Nativity	60,64,75,85			
country of birth	63			
Occupations	68,78,88			
Poverty	82,92			
Transportation	65,75,85			

Decennial Year	1980
Census	Twentieth Decennial Census
Volume	Volume I Chapter D Part 1
Title	1980 Census of Population Characteristics of the Population Detailed Population Characteristics United States Summary Sec. A, B1, B2 and C
Publication	Department of Commerce, Bureau of the Census Washington, DC: Government Printing Office
Date	1984
Classifications	
Supt. of Documents	C 3.223/8:980/v.1/D 1/pt. 1/sec. A, B1 and 2, C
Library of Congress	HA 201.1980.A13 v.1 ch.D pt.1 sec. A, B1 & 2, C
card	81-607950
Dewey	312.0973
Census designation	PC80-1-D-1
Microforms	
A.S.I.	ASI 1984 2531-4.1
Pages	vi, 636, 59 app. pages
Maps, illustrations	None
Notes	Tables 194-367 are in this four-section part, which provides extensive demographic details for the various social and economic characteristics.

Section A has Tables 253-310 with United States data. Section B1 has Tables 311-326, and B2 has Tables 327-341 with data for Census Regions. Section C has Tables 342-367 with data for Standard Metropolitan Statistical Areas. |

1980
Volume I Characteristics of the Population Chapter D Detailed
Population Characteristics Part 1 United States Summary
Sections A, B1 and 2, and C

	Sec. A United States	*Sec. B Regions	Sec. C SCSAs
Demographic Characteristics			
Aggregate population	253	311	342

Age
  Note: Nearly all tables with
  age data also include sex as
  a variable.
	255,258-262,
	264-266,268-273,
	280,289,293,296-
	298,303,304,306-
	308,310
		311,313-
		323,335,
		337,338,
		340
			344-352,
			356,358,
			363-365

Race	253,255,259-266, 268-275,277-282, 286-288,290,291, 293-304,306-310	311,313, 315-319, 321-325, 327-330, 332,333, 335-340	
Spanish origin	253,255,259-266, 268-288,290,291, 293,294,296-304, 306-310	311,313, 315-319, 321-325	

Sex
  Note: Sex is included as a
  variable in nearly every age
  table, plus these tables.
	267,276-282,285-
	288,290,291,294,
	295,301,303,309
		324,325,
		327-333
			353,354,
			356

Marital status	255,264,267	313,317, 320	344
Social and Economic Characteristics			
Citizenship	253-256	311,312, 314	342

*Section B, Regions, is in two parts. The first includes Tables 311-
326. The second part includes Tables 327-341.

1980
Volume I Characteristics of the Population Chapter D Detailed
Population Characteristics Part 1 United States Summary
Sections A, B1 and 2, and C

	Sec. A United States	Sec. B Regions	Sec. C SCSAs
Education			
School enrollment			
by age	258,260,261		
by sex	260		
by family income	261		
by veteran status	263		
by poverty status	261		
Years of school completed	255,258,262, 282,296,306	313,316, 320,334, 336	360
Employment	258,276,278, 279,280,282- 285,287-289	313,321, 323-327, 329,331	352,354, 357
Place of work/re SMSA, state	291,292	331	
Class of employer	279,288		
Families	255,267-269, 309	313,335, 336,338- 340	345,347, 358,359, 361,362, 366,367
Fertility	255,270,271	313,320	
Households	255,256,294, 301-303	313,318, 320,337, 338	345-347, 350,361- 363
Group quarters	266	313,319	
Immigration			
Years since, by country of emigration	254,255	312,313, 326	342
Income	258,281,290, 293-303	332-336	356-363
Of unrelated individuals	298		
Industry	283-289	326-329, 340	354-355
Historic from 1970			330

1980
Volume I Characteristics of the Population   Chapter D Detailed
Population Characteristics   Part 1 United States Summary
Sections A, B1 and 2, and C

	Sec. A United States	Sec. B Regions	Sec. C SCSAs
Labor force	258,272-275, 277,281,285, 286,290	313,320- 322,330, 331,333, 336	348-351, 353,355, 357,360
Language			
Spoken at home	255-258	314	343
Ability to speak English	255,256	314	343
Migration	253,258,259	311,312, 315	
Military/veterans			
Veterans	259,263,291	312	
by period of service	263		
Nativity	253-255	311-313	
General nativity	253,254	311,312	
Specific	254	313	
born in Puerto Rico		311,312	
Occupations	276-284,291, 292,305	319,320, 323-325, 328	352,353
Detailed occupation by sex	276		
historic from 1970	276		
Poverty	258,304-310	338-341	364-367
Type income	307	339	
With Social Security,			
public assistance	307,308	339	
Transportation	291,292	331	
Means, to work	291,292	331	

Decennial Year	1980
Census	Twentieth Decennial Census
Volume	Volume I Chapter D Parts 2-55
Title	1980 Census of Population Characteristics of the Population Detailed Population Characteristics States and Outlying Areas
Publication	Department of Commerce, Bureau of the Census Washington, DC: Government Printing Office
Date	1983, 1984, 1985

Classifications

Supt. of Documents	C 3.223/8:980/v.1/D 2-53, 55
Library of Congress	HA 215.1980.A13 v.1 ch.D pts.2-53, 55
card	81-607950
Dewey	312.0973
Census designation	PC80-1-D2-53, 55

Microforms

A.S.I.	ASI 1983, 1984, 1985 2531-4.2 through 2531-4.55
Pages	Vary
Maps, illustrations	None
Notes	This chapter includes Tables 194-251. They contain socioeconomic data classified by demographic factors and are limited to data for the state and for SMSA's. There are no tables for counties or places.

Only 53 parts are included in this set of reports, with Puerto Rico (pt. 53) and the Virgin Islands (Pt. 55) the only outlying areas for which reports were published.

1980
Volume I Characteristics of the Population Chapter D Detailed
Population Characteristics Parts 2-55 States and Outlying Areas

	State	SMSA's of 250,000
Demographic Characteristics		
Aggregate population	194	
Age	194	
By race and Spanish origin	194,200,201,203,205, 207,210,211,213-216, 221,234,237-239,244, 245,247-251	
by sex	200,201,203,205-207, 213,214,221,234,237-239, 244,245,247,248,251	
Race	194,202,240,241,243	
See Age above and Sex below Note that all tables by race in this Chapter also show data by Spanish origin.		
Spanish origin	194,202,240,241,243	
Sex	196	
By race and Spanish origin	216,219,220,222,223, 225,227-229,231,235- 239,244,245,247,248	216,219,220, 222,227-229, 231,232,234- 239,247,249
Marital status	196,205,208	205,208,247
By age, race and Spanish origin	205	205
Social and Economic Characteristics		
Citizenship		
Foreign born by citizenship status	194	
by country of birth	195	195
Citizens 18+ years by language spoken at home	197	

1980
Volume I Characteristics of the Population Chapter D Detailed
Population Characteristics Parts 2-55 States and Outlying Areas

	State	SMSAs of 250,000
Education		
School enrollment		
by age, sex, race and Spanish origin	201	
of related children by age, race, Spanish origin, by type of school and by family income		
of veterans	204	
Years of school completed		
by age, sex, race and Spanish origin	203	203
by income	237	237
by poverty status	247	247
Employment/unemployment	236	236
Hours worked - by sex, race and Spanish origin	229	229
Weeks worked 1979	214	214
By industry	229	229
Of class of employer	229	229
Of unpaid family workers	229	229
Place of work		
by industry	233	233
by occupation	232	232
Families	198,208	208
By age, race and Spanish origin	210	210
Subfamilies, unrelated individ-uduals, unmarried couples	208	208
By type, number and age of children	209	209
Family income	238,240	238,240
Fertility		
Children ever born		
to women 15+ years	211	
to women 15-44 years, rate	212	

1980
Volume I Characteristics of the Population Chapter D Detailed
Population Characteristics Parts 2-55 States and Outlying Areas

	State	SMSAs of 250,000
Households		
By age and sex, by race and Spanish origin	206	206
Group quarters		
by age and sex, by race and Spanish origin	207	207
Immigration		
Year of immigration by country of birth	195	195
Since 1970, by social characteristics and area of birth	196	
Income	234-240	234-244
By age and sex, by race and Spanish origin	234	234
By years of school completed	237	237
Family income	238	238
by family size	240	240
by married couple families	241	241
Of unrelated individuals by age	239	239
By household relationships	235	235
other than married couples	242	242
by household size	244	244
By income type	243	243
By labor force status	236	236
Industry	224-227	227-231
Detailed industry by sex	226	
Of experienced labor force	227	227
by earnings	231	231
Of employed person	228	228
by age and sex	230	230
By class of employer	229	229
Institutional population	207,208	207,208
By type of institution	208	208
By marital status	208	208
Labor force	213-216	213-216
By age, sex, race and Spanish origin, and employment status	213	213

	State	SMSAs of 250,000
Labor force (continued)		
By household type and presence of children	215	215
Married couple families	216	216
Language		
Spoken at home		
by age groups and sex	197,198	198
by citizenship	197	
by ability to speak English	197	
Ability to speak English	197	
by age, mobility, education, labor force status and occupation	199	
by Spanish language spoken at home	199	
Migration/mobility		
Born in state of residence or elsewhere, by age and race	194	
Residence in 1975 by age, sex, race and Spanish origin	200	
Nativity		
General nativity by age, race and Spanish origin	194	
Place of birth by age, race and Spanish origin	194	
Foreign born by country of birth	195	195
by year of immigration	195,196	195
Foreign born who immigrated after 1970, by area of birth		
by age, sex, marital status	196	
by family status	196	
by household type	196	
by fertility	196	
by education	196	
by language	196	
by employment	196	
by income and poverty status	196	
by labor force status	196	
by occupation	196	

212

1980
Volume I Characteristics of the Population Chapter D Detailed
Population Characteristics Parts 2-55 States and Outlying Areas

	State	SMSAs of 250,000
Occupations	217-225	219-222
By age, sex, race and Spanish origin	221	221
Detailed occupation by sex		
by employment status	217	
historic from 1970	217	
by race and Spanish origin	219	219
of experienced labor force	218	
By class of employer	220	220
By hours worked	220	220
Of employed persons by age, sex, race and Spanish origin	221	221
by education	223	
by industry	224,225	
Of experienced labor force by earnings in 1979	222	222
Poverty	245-251	245-251
Persons by poverty status	245	245
Families and unrelated individuals by social characteristics	246-251	246-251
Transportation		
By place of work		232

Apportionment, Geography

Inside/outside central cities		
By residence and place of work		232
Rural		
By marital status	205,208	
By education	203,237	
By family status	208-210	
By household type	206,207	
Institutional population	207	

Decennial Year   1980

Census   Twentieth Decennial Census

Volume   Volume II   Subject Reports   Part 1

Titles   1 D   American Indians, Eskimos, and Aleuts on
                                  Identified Reservations and in the
                                  Historic Areas of Oklahoma (Excluding
                                  Urbanized Areas)
                            1 E   Asian and Pacific Islander Population in
                                  the United States: 1980

Publication   Department of Commerce, Bureau of the Census
                            Washington, DC: Government Printing Office

Date   Part 1 D Sec 1 1985, Sec 2 1986;   Part 1 E 1988

Classifications

  Supt. of Documents   C 3.223/10:980/v.2/pt.1 D pts.1 and 2, 1 E

  Library of Congress   HA 201.B.1980k v.2 pt.1D pts.1 and 2, pt.1 E

   card   81-607939

  Dewey   312.0973

  Census designation   PC80-2-1 D pts.1 and 2; pt. 1 E

Microforms

  A.S.I.   Part 1 D Sec. 1 ASI 1985 2533-13.1; Sec. 2 ASI
                            1986 2533-13.2;   Part 1 E not yet on ASI fiche

Pages   Part 1 D Sec.1 ix, 130, 6a; Sec. 2 x, 190,
                            47a;   Part 1 E   xii, 952

Maps, illustration   One map of Oklahoma in section of Part 1 D.

Notes   Data are provided in the two-section Part 1 D
                            on demographic and socioeconomic character-
                            istics of these populations. It is also pro-
                            vided on Indian use of health services, the
                            only 1980 report covering this subject. Data
                            are based on a 75 percent sample. Part 1 E was
                            published in 1988. Subject reports A, B, C, F
                            and G were planned but not published.

1980
Volume II Subject Reports Part 1 D Sections 1 and 2 and Part 1 E

	Part 1 D	Part 1 E
Demographic Characteristics		
Aggregate population	x	x
Limited to persons resident on reservations and in the Historic Areas of Oklahoma (excluding urbanized areas)	x	
Age	x	x
Race	x	x
American Indians	x	
tribal enrollment	x	
Eskimos	x	
Aleuts	x	
Asian and Pacific Islanders		x
Sex	x	x
Marital status	x	x
Social and Economic Characteristics		
Citizenship		x
Education		
School enrollment	x	x
Years of school completed	x	x
Employment/unemployment	x	x
Families	x	x
Fertility		x
Health	x	
Households	x	x
Housing	x	

1980
Volume II Subject Reports Part 1 D Sections 1 and 2 and Part 1 E

	Part 1 D	Part 1 E
Immigration		x
Income	x	x
Industry	x	
Labor Force	x	x
Language		x
Migration/mobility	x	
Time on reservation	x	
Military/veterans		x
Nativity		x
Occupations	x	x
Poverty	x	x

Apportionment, Geography

Reservations and Oklahoma Historic Areas	x	
Standard Federal Administrative Areas	x	
Inside/outside SMSA's		x

Decennial Year	1980
Census	Twentieth Decennial Census
Volume	Volume II Subject Reports Part 2
Title	2 A Geographical Mobility for States and the Nation 2 C Geographical Mobility for Metropolitan Areas
Publication	Department of Commerce, Bureau of the Census Washington, DC: Government Printing Office
Date	Part 2 A 1985; Part 2 C 1984

Classifications

Supt. of Documents	C 3.223/10:980/v.2/pts.2 A and C
Library of Congress	HA 201.1980k. v.2 pts.2 A and C
card	81-607939
Dewey	312.0973
Census designation	PC80-2-2 A and C

Microforms

A.S.I.	Part 2 A ASI 1985 2533-12; Part 2 C ASI 1984 2533-8
Pages	Part 2 A viii, 874, 19a; Part 2 C viii, 725, 38a pages
Maps, illustrations	Part 2 A, 1 map; Part 2 C, 2 maps.
Notes	Part 2 A provides information on demographic and socioeconomic characteristics of the mobile population and interstate migration between 1975 and 1980.
	Part 2 C provides demographic and socioeconomic data on the population which moved into or out of, or within Standard Metropolitan Statistical Areas between 1975 and 1980. This part includes details on each named SMSA.
	Part 2 B was planned but not published.

1980
Volume II Subject Reports Parts 2 A and C

	Part A	Part C
Demographic Characteristics		
Aggregate population		
Limited to persons 5+ years	x	x
Age	x	x
Race	x	x
Spanish origin	x	x
Sex	x	x
Marital status	x	
Social and Economic Characteristics		
Education		
Years of school completed	x	x
In college, 1975 or 1980	x	x
Households	x	x
Group quarters	x	
Income	x	x
Industry	x	
Institutional population	x	
Labor force	x	
Migration/mobility	x	x
Military/veterans		
Armed forces 1975 or 1980	x	x
Occupations	x	x

1980
Volume II Subject Reports Parts 2 A and C

	Part A	Part C
<u>Apportionment,Geography</u>		
Regions	x	
Divisions	x	
States	x	
Standard Metropolitan Statistical Areas		x

Decennial Year	1980
Census	Twentieth Decennial Census
Volume	Volume II Subject Reports Part 4
Title	4 B Living Arrangements of Children and Adults 4 C Marital Characteristics 4 D Persons in Institutions and Other Group Quarters
Publication	Department of Commerce, Bureau of the Census Washington, DC: Government Printing Office
Date	Parts 4 B and C, 1985; Part 4 D, 1984
Classifications	
Supt. of Documents	C 3.223/10:980/v.2/pts.4 B, C, D
Library of Congress	HA 201.1980k v.2 pts.4 B, C, D
card	81-607939
Dewey	312.0973
Census designation	PC80-2-4 B, C, D
Microforms	
A.S.I.	Part 4 B ASI 1985 2533-10; Part 4 C ASI 1985 2533-6; Part 4 D ASI 1984 2533-5
Pages	Part 4 B viii, 103, 35a; Part 4 C vii, 319, 35a; Part 4 D xi, 857, 39a pages
Maps, illustrations	None
Notes	Part 4 B provides demographic and socioeconomic data on both adults and children. Part 4 C provides demographic and socioeconomic data on husbands and wives, on marital status and history, as well as information on unmarried individuals. Part 4 D provides demographic and socioeconomic data on institutionalized persons as well as data on the institutions. Part 4 A was planned but not published.

1980
Volume II Subject Reports Parts 4 B, C and D

	Part B	Part C	Part D
Demographic Characteristics			
Aggregate population			
Limited to persons 15+ years		x	
Limited to inmates of institutions and			
persons in group quarters			x
Age	x	x	x
Age differences of husband and wife		x	
Race	x	x	x
Spanish origin	x	x	x
Sex	x	x	x
Marital status	x	x	x
Marital history	x	x	x
Marriage rate		x	
Unmarried couples	x		
Social and Economic Characteristics			
Disabilities			x
Education			
School enrollment	x		x
Years of school completed	x	x	x
Employment/unemployment		x	
Families	x		
Foster children	x		
Households	x		
Group quarters	x		
Noninstitutional group quarters	x		x
Income	x	x	x
Wife/husband comparison	x		
Labor force	x		

1980
Volume II   Subject Reports   Parts 4 B, C and D

	Part B	Part C	Part D
Migration/mobility	x		x
Military/veterans Veterans by period of service			x
Nativity		x	x
By U.S. region		x	
Specific by county of birth			x
Occupations		x	x

Apportionment, Geography

Urban/rural			x
Regions			x
States			x
Standard Metropolitan Statistical Areas			x
Inside/outside			x
Cities, places, towns, townships			x

Decennial Year	1980
Census	Twentieth Decennial Census
Volume	Volume II Subject Reports Parts 6 C, D and E
Titles	Part 6 C Journey to Work: Metropolitan Commuting Flows Part 6 D Journey to Work: Characteristics of Workers in Metropolitan Areas Sections 1, 2, 3 Part 6 E Place of Work
Publication	Department of Commerce, Bureau of the Census Washington, DC: Government Printing Office
Date	1984

Classifications

Supt. of Documents	C 3.223/10:980/v.2/pts.6 C, D, E
Library of Congress	HA 201.1980k v.2 pts.6 C, D, E
card	81-607939
Dewey	312.0973
Census designation	PC80-2-6 C, D, E

Microforms

A.S.I.	Part 6 C ASI 1984 2533-1; Part 6 D ASI 1985 2533-7; Part 6 E ASI 1984 2533-2
Pages	Part 6 C 556, 31a; Part 6 D, 3 sections 1177, 960, 86537a; Part 6 E 996, 37a pages
Maps, illustrations	None
Notes	Part 6 C relates residence to place of work and provides data for each specific SMSA. Part 6 D, which was published in 3 sections, provides demographic and socioeconomic data on those who work in metropolitan areas, with information for each SMSA. Part 6 E relates occupation and industry to travel time and method of reaching the place of work. Parts 6 A and 6 B were planned but not published.

1980
Volume II   Subject Reports   Parts 6 C, D and E

	Part C	Part D	Part E
Demographic Characteristics			
Aggregate population			
Limited to workers 16+ years	x	x	x
Age		x	x
Race		x	x
Spanish origin		x	x
Sex		x	x
Marital status			x
Social and Economic Characteristics			
Education			
Years of school completed		x	x
Employment/unemployment		x	x
Class of employer		x	x
Households		x	x
Group quarters		x	x
Income		x	x
Industry		x	x
Labor force		x	
Military/veterans			
In armed forces		x	x
Occupations		x	x
Transportation/journey to work	x	x	x
Place of residence/place of work	x		

1980
Volume II   Subject Reports   Parts 6 C, D and E

	Part C	Part D	Part E
Social and Economic Characteristics			
Regions	x	x	
Standard Metropolitan Statistical Areas Each SMSA is listed by name, and data are provided for the number of workers by place of residence and place of work.	x	x	

Decennial Year	1980
Census	Twentieth Decennial Census
Volume	Volume II Subject Reports Part 7
Title	7 C Occupation by Industry
Publication	Department of Commerce, Bureau of the Census Washington, DC: Government Printing Office
Date	1984

Classifications

Supt. of Documents	C 3.223/10:980/v.2/pt.7 C
Library of Congress	HA 201.1980 v.2 pt.7 C
card	81-607939
Dewey	312.0973
Census designation	PC80-2-7 C

Microforms

A.S.I.	Part 7 C ASI 1985 2533-3
Pages	Part 7 C v, 664, 42a pages
Maps, illustrations	None
Notes	This is the only volume published on the subjects of industry and occupations. Most of the data are on those two subjects, classified by sex, and race and Spanish origin.
	Parts 7 A, 7 B and 7 D were planned but not published.

Part 7 C

Demographic Characteristics

Age
  Limited to persons of 16+ years

Race   x

Spanish origin   x

Sex   x

Social and Economic Characteristics

Education
  Percent high school graduates   x
  Percent 4+ years college   x

Employment/unemployment   x
  Self-employed   x

Income   x

Industry   x
  Last industry of those unemployed   x

Occupations   x

Decennial Year	1980
Census	Twentieth Decennial Census
Volume	Volume II Subject Reports Part 8
Titles	8 B Earnings by Occupation and Education
	8 D Poverty Areas in Large Cities
	8 Da Addendum
Publication	Department of Commerce, Bureau of the Census Washington, DC: Government Printing Office
Date	Part 8 B 1984; Parts 8 D and 8 Da 1985

Classifications

Supt. of Documents	C 3.223/10:980/v.2/pts.8 B, D, Da
Library of Congress	HA 201.1980k v.2 pts.8 B, D, Da
card	81-607939
Dewey	312.0973
Census designation	PC80-2-8 B, D, Da

Microforms

A.S.I.	Part 8 B ASI 1984 2533-4; Part 8 D ASI 1985 2533-9
Pages	Part 8 B v, 498, 37a; Part 8 D vi, 700, 40a; Part 8 Da appendix pages 13-17 only, omitted from original printing
Maps, illustrations	None
Notes	Part 8 B provides data on incomes by education for about 500 occupations. Part 8 D provides summary social and economic data for 100 central cities.
	Parts 8 A and 8 C were planned but not published

1980
Volume II Subject Reports Parts 8 B and D

	Part B	Part D
Demographic Characteristics		
Aggregate population		
Population restricted to persons aged 18 years and in the recent experienced labor force with earnings	x	
Population of persons in SMSA's with the 100 largest central cities		x
Age	x	x
Race	x	x
Spanish Origin	x	x
Sex	x	x
Social and Economic Characteristics		
Education		
School enrollment		x
Years of school completed	x	x
Employment/Unemployment	x	x
Families		x
Households		x
Female householder, no husband present		x
Householder 65+ years		x
Group quarters		x
Housing		x
Income	x	x
By type		x
Labor force	x	x
Occupations	x	
Poverty		x

Decennial Year	1980
Census	Twentieth Decennial Census
Volume	Volume II Subject Reports Part 9
Title	9 C Characteristics of the Rural and Farm-Related Population
Publication	Department of Commerce, Bureau of the Census Washington, DC: Government Printing Office
Date	1985

Classifications

Supt. of Documents	C 3.223/10:980/v.2/pt.9 C
Library of Congress	HA 201.1980k v.2 pt.9 C
card	81-607939
Dewey	312.0973
Census designation	PC80-2-9 C

Microforms

A.S.I.	Part 9 C ASI 1985 2533-11
Pages	Part 9 C vi, 195, 37a pages
Maps, illustrations	No maps or illustrations
Notes	Data are for the U.S. and for regions, and are restricted to the population living on farms and/or receiving farm self-employment income, and/or employed in agriculture. There are 7 tables.
	Parts 9 A, B, D, E and F were planned but not published.

1980
Volume II Subject Reports Part 9 C

	Part 9 C

Demographic Characteristics

Aggregate population
  Restricted to persons living on farms, receiving farm
    self-employment income, and/or employed in agriculture   x

Age   x

Race   x

Spanish origin   x

Sex   x

Marital status   x

Social and Economic Characteristics

Education
  Years of school completed   x

Employment/unemployment
  Persons employed in agriculture   x
  Weeks worked in 1979 by householder/spouse   x

Families
  Persons per family   x
  Workers per family   x

Farmers/Farms   x
  By 1970 definition of farms   x

Fertility   x

Households   x
  Family/nonfamily householder   x
  With a farm operator or manager   x
  With farm self-employment income   x

Housing   x

1980
Volume II Subject Reports Part 9 C

	Part 9 C
Income	
Farm self-employment income, percent of income	x
Type income	x
Industry	x
Labor force status	x
Migration/mobility	
Residence in 1975	x
Year moved into present house	x
Occupations	
Householder/spouse	x
Poverty	x
Transportation/journey to work	
Time of travel to work	x
Apportionment, Geography	
Rural/rural farm	x
Regions	x

Subject Reports Planned and Having Numbers Assigned
List of Those Published and Those Cancelled

Below is a list of the subject reports planned for publication following the 1980 Census. Most of the planned reports were on subjects
of reports in earlier censuses. Of the total planned, only 14 were
published.

Number	Title	Publ.	Cancld.
1 A	Black Population		x
1 B	Persons of Spanish Origin or Surname		x
1 C	American Indians, Eskimos, and Aleuts in the United States		x
1 D	American Indians, Eskimos, and Aleuts on Identified Reservations and in the Historic Areas of Oklahoma	x	
1 E	Asian and Pacific Islander Population of the United States: 1980	x	
1 F	Persons Born in Foreign Countries		x
1 G	Language Usage in the United States		x
2 A	Geographical Mobility for States and the Nation	x	
2 B	Lifetime and Recent Migration		x
2 C	Geographical Mobility for Metropolitan Areas	x	
3 A	Fertility		x
4 A	Household and Family Composition		x
4 B	Living Arrangments of Children and Adults	x	
4 C	Marital Characteristics	x	
4 D	Persons in Institutions and Other Group Quarters	x	
5 A,B,C	Education		x
6 A	Labor Force Status and Work Experience		x
6 B	Persons Not Employed		x
6 C	Journey to Work: Metropolitan Commuting Flows	x	
6 D	Journey to Work: Characteristics of Workers in Metropolitan Areas	x	
6 E	Place of Work	x	

1980
Subject Reports Planned

Number	Title	Publ.	Cancld.
7 A	Occupational Characteristics		x
7 B	IndustrialCharacteristics		x
7 C	Occupation by Industry	x	
7 D	Government Workers		x
8 A	Sources and Structure of Household and Family Income		x
8 B	Earnings by Occupation and Education	x	
8 C	Characteristics of the Poverty Population		x
8 D	Poverty Areas in Large Cities and Addendum	x	
9 A	Characteristics of Metropolitan Population		x
9 B	Persons by Census Tract Characteristics		x
9 C	Characteristics of the Rural and Farm-Related Population	x	
9 D	Older Population		x
9 E	Women		x
9 F	Veterans		x

Decennial Year   1980

Census   Twentieth Decennial Census

Volume   ·   Supplementary Report 1

Title   Age, Sex, Race, and Spanish Origin of the
                            Population by Regions, Divisions, and States:
                            1980

Publication   Department of Commerce, Bureau of the Census
                            Washington, DC: Government Printing Office

Date   1981

Classifications

   Supt. of Documents   C 3.223/12:980-S 1-1

   Library of Congress   HA 201.1980.B A569x

      card   84-602973

   Dewey   312.0973

   Census designation   PC80-S1-1

Microforms

   A.S.I.   ASI 1981 2535-1.1

Pages   6 pages

Maps, illustrations   None

Notes   This is the first of a very useful series of
                            supplementary reports. Each has an essay on
                            the first few pages, followed by a number of
                            tables of data on the subjects indicated in
                            the titles.

                            This report provides information on the five
                            major racial groups in the United States, as
                            well as on the population of Spanish origin.

1980
Supplementary Report 1 Age, Sex, Race, and Spanish Origin of the Population by Regions, Divisions, and States: 1980

	U.S.	Regions	Divisions	States
Demographic Characteristics				
Aggregate population	1,2	2	2	2
Age				
5 year age groups	1	2	2	2
by race, by sex	1			
Race	1,3	3	3	3
By age, by sex for				
White	1	3	3	3
Black	1	3	3	3
American Indian, Eskimo and Aleut	1	3	3	3
Asian and Pacific Islander	1	3	3	3
Spanish origin				
By age, by sex	1			
Sex	3	3	3	3

Decennial Year	1980
Census	Twentieth Decennial Census
Volume	Supplementary Report 2
Title	Population and Households by States and Counties: 1980
Publication	Department of Commerce, Bureau of the Census Washington, DC: Government Printing Office
Date	1981

Classifications

Supt. of Documents	C 3.223/12:980-S 1-2
Library of Congress	HA 201.1980.B A569x
card	84-602973
Dewey	312.0973
Census designation	PC80-S1-2

Microforms

A.S.I.	ASI 1981 2535-1.2
Pages	23 pages
Maps, illustrations	None
Notes	There is only one table in this report. It is arranged alphabetically by state and county, showing the number of persons in households and group quarters, the number of households, and persons per household. The 1980 definition of households and group quarters is found on page 2.

1980
Supplementary Report 2 Population and Households by States and Counties: 1980

	States	Counties
Demographic Characteristics		
Aggregate population	1	1
Social and Economic Characteristics		
Households		
Number households	1	1
Number persons in households	1	1
Persons per household	1	1
Persons in group quarters	1	1

Decennial Year	1980
Census	Twentieth Decennial Census
Volume	Supplementary Report 3
Title	Race of the Population by States: 1980
Publication	Department of Commerce, Bureau of the Census Washington, DC: Government Printing Office
Date	1981

Classifications

Supt. of Documents	C 3.223/12:980-S 1-3
Library of Congress	HA 201.1980.B A569x
card	84-602973
Dewey	312.0973
Census designation	PC80-S1-3

Microforms

A.S.I.	ASI 1981 2535-1.3
Pages	14 pages
Maps, illustrations	None
Notes	This report includes total, not sample, data on 15 racial groups. It is more detailed than Supplementary Report 1. The first pages contain extensive definitions and explanations. A facsimile of the questionnaire item on race as well as instructions to respondents are included.

1980
Supplementary Report 3   Race of the Population by States: 1980

	United States	Regions, Divisions	States
Demographic Characteristics			
Aggregate population	1,3	1,3	1,3
Race			
White, Black, American Indian, Eskimo, Aleut, Chinese, Filipino, Japanese, Asian Indian, Korean, Vietnamese, Hawaiian, Samoan, Guamanian, Other	1	1	1
Percent distribution	2	2	2
Historic from 1970	3	3	3
percent distribution	4	4	4
Selected states			
Black - 1980 and 1970, percent, and 1980 rank	5		5
American Indian - 1980 and 1970, percent, and 1980 rank	6		6
Asian and Pacific Islander - 1980 percent and rank	7		7
Chinese - 1980, percent and rank	7		7
Filipino - 1980, percent and rank	7		7
Japanese - 1980, percent and rank	7		7
Korean - 1980, percent and rank	7		7
Asian Indian - 1980, percent	8		8
Hawaiian - 1980, percent	8		8
Vietnamese - 1980, percent	8		8

Decennial Year	1980
Census	Twentieth Decennial Census
Volume	Supplementary Report 4
Title	Population and Households for Census Designated Places: 1980
Publication	Department of Commerce, Bureau of the Census Washington, DC: Government Printing Office
Date	1981

Classifications

Supt. of Documents	C 3.223/12:980-S 1-4
Library of Congress	HA 201.1980.B A569x
card	84-602973
Dewey	312.0973
Census designation	PC80-S1-4

Microforms

A.S.I.	ASI 1981 2535-1.4
Pages	42 pages
Maps, illustrations	None
Notes	This report provides data for "densely settled population concentrations that are not separately incorporated as cities, villages, etc." The definition of Census Designated Places is found on page 1. It requires a minimum of 1,000 persons outside of urbanized places. There were 3.434 such places in 1980. There is but a single table of places listed by state and county in alphabetical order. The four columns show persons, households, persons in households, and persons per household.

1980
**Supplementary Report 4   Population and Households for Census
Designated Places: 1980**

	Census Designated Places*

Demographic Characteristics

Aggregate population of Census Designated
  Places by state and county   1

Social and Economic Characteristics

Households
  Number households   1
  Persons in households   1
  Persons per household   1

---

*"Census Designated Places" are places delineated by the Census
Bureau to make it possible to provide census data for densely
settled population concentrations that are not separately incorporated as cities, villages or other named jurisdictions.
The term corresponds to the term "unincorporated places" used
in the 1950, 1960 and 1970 censuses.

Decennial Year	1980
Census	Twentieth Decennial Census
Volume	Supplementary Report 5
Title	Standard Metropolitan Statistical Areas and Standard Consolidated Statistical Areas: 1980
Publication	Department of Commerce, Bureau of the Census Washington, DC: Government Printing Office
Date	1981

Classifications

Supt. of Documents	C 3.223/12:980-S 1-5
Library of Congress	HA 201.1980.B A569x
card	84-602973
Dewey	312.0973
Census designation	PC80-S1-5

Microforms

A.S.I.	ASI 1981 2535-1.5
Pages	68 pages
Maps, illustrations	None
Notes	This report presents population data on the 323 Standard Metropolitan Statistical Areas and the 17 Standard Consolidated Statistical Areas and their component parts for 1980. The appendix lists the names of each, together with other designation codes.

1980
**Supplementary Report 5   Standard Metropolitan Statistical Areas
and Standard Consolidated Statistical Areas: 1980**

	United States	SCSAs	SMSAs	Component Parts
Demographic Characteristics				
Aggregate population	3	2,4	1,4	1
Historic from 1970	3	2,4	4	
Rank - 1980 and 1970		4	4	
Race				
White	3	2	1,2	1
Black	3	2	1,2	1
American Indian, Eskimo, Aleut	3	2	1,2	1
Asian, Pacific Islander	3	2	1,2	1
Spanish origin	3	2	1,2	1
Social and Economic Characteristics				
Households		7	7	7
Persons in households		7	7	7
Persons per household		7	7	7
Persons in group quarters		7	7	7
In metropolitan and nonmetropolitan areas	F			
Housing				
Number units	3	2	1,2	1
Historic from 1970	3	2	1,2	1
Apportionment, Geography				
Metropolitan and nonmetropolitan population	5			
Historic from 1950	A			
Percent change from 1940	B			
Inside/outside SMSAs	3,5			
Inside/outside central cities	3,6			
by race and Spanish origin	3,E			
SMSAs	D			
Historic from 1950	D			
Number central cities	D			

Decennial Year	1980
Census	Twentieth Decennial Census
Volume	Supplementary Report 6
Title	Nonpermanent Residents by States and Selected Counties and Incorporated Places: 1980
Publication	Department of Commerce, Bureau of the Census Washington, DC: Government Printing Office
Date	1982

Classifications

Supt. of Documents	C 3.223/12:980-S 1-6
Library of Congress	HA 201.1980.B A569x
card	84-602973
Dewey	312.0973
Census designation	PC80-S1-6

Microforms

A.S.I.	ASI 1982 2535-1.6
Pages	29 pages
Maps, illustrations	None
Notes	This is the first time the Census Bureau has published data on this subject, contrasting the place of residence on the census date with the usual place of residence. Tables in the introductory text provide valuable information not hitherto available.

1980
Supplementary Report 6 Nonpermanent Residents by States and
Selected Counties and Incorporated Places: 1980

	United States	States	Selected Counties	Incor. Places
Demographic Characteristics				
Aggregate population				
Report limited to persons in nonpermanent households on date of census, April 1, 1980, by state of usual residence	2	2		
Counties with 500+ persons of nonpermanent residence, by region of usual residence		4	4	
Incorporated places with 500+ persons of nonpermanent residence, by region of usual residence		6		6
States with most nonpermanent residents	A	A		
nonpermanent residents per 1,000 permanent residents	A	A		
Permanent residents living elsewhere, by state	B	B		
Age				
Age distribution of persons in nonpermanent households	8	8	8	
by sex	8	8	8	
Median age of persons in non-permanent households	C	C		
Persons in one-person households	7	7	7	
Multiperson households by number of members	7	7	7	
Sex	8	8	8	

1980
Supplementary Report 6 Nonpermanent Residents by States and
Selected Counties and Incorporated Places: 1980

	United States	States	Selected Counties	Incor. Places
Social and Economic Characteristics				
Households				
Number of nonpermanent households	1	1		
by state of usual residence	1	1		
by region of usual residence		3	3	
one-person households	7	7	7	
incorporated places with 500+				
nonpermanent households		5		5
Average size of nonpermanent				
households	C	C		
Multiperson households by age of				
members	7	7	7	
percent with all persons 65+				
years	C	C		
percent with all persons 15-24				
years	C	C		
By size of household	9	9	9	

Decennial Census	1980
Census	Twentieth Decennial Census
Volume	Supplementary Report 7
Title	Persons of Spanish Origin by State: 1980
Publication	Department of Commerce, Bureau of the Census Washington, DC: Government Printing Office
Date	1982

Classifications

Supt. of Documents	C 3.223/12:980-S 1-7
Library of Congress	HA 201.1980.B A569x
card	84-602973
Dewey	312.0973
Census designation	PC80-S1-7

Microforms

A.S.I.	ASI 1982 2535-1.7
Pages	17 pages
Maps, illustrations	None
Notes	For the first time, in the 1980 Census, the question "Is this person of Spanish/Hispanic origin or descent?" was asked of all persons. Those replying in the affirmative are shown as Mexican, Puerto Rican, Cuban or "other Spanish."
	A separate section of the report provides a preliminary evaluation of responses in the Mexican origin category.

1980
Supplementary Report 7 Persons of Spanish Origin by State: 1980

	United States	Regions, Divisions	States
Demographic Characteristics			
Aggregate population	1	1	1
Report limited to persons of Spanish origin	1	1	1
Race			
Race of persons of Spanish origin	4	4	4
percent	5	5	5
Race of persons not of Spanish origin	4	4	4
percent	5	5	5
Spanish origin	1	1	1
Historic from 1970	p.2		
rank, selected states, 1980 and 1970	6		6
Type of Spanish origin			
Mexican	1	1	1
rank, selected states, 1980 and 1970		7	7
Puerto Rican	1	1	1
rank, selected states, 1980 and 1970		8	8
Cuban	1	1	1
rank, selected states, 1980 and 1970		9	9
other Spanish	1	1	1
Percent each type	2	2	2
Percent distribution	3	3	3

Decennial Year	1980
Census	Twentieth Decennial Census
Volume	Supplementary Report 8
Title	Detailed Occupation and Years of School Completed by Age, for the Civilian Labor Force by Sex, Race, and Spanish Origin: 1980
Publication	Department of Commerce, Bureau of the Census Washington, DC: Government Printing Office
Date	1983

Classifications

Supt. of Documents	C 3.223/12:980-S 1-8
Library of Congress	HA 201.1980.B A569x
card	84-602973
Dewey	312.0973
Census designation	PC80-S1-8

Microforms

A.S.I.	ASI 1983 2535-1.8
Pages	30 pages
Maps, illustrations	None
Notes	This report has four tables, the first two based on census occupational classifications, and the other two on years of school completed by race and Spanish origin.
	It provides data for the Census Bureau's Equal Opportunity Special File, designed to assist in affirmative action efforts.

1980
Supplementary Report 8 Detailed Occupation and Years of School
Completed by Age, for the Civilian Labor Force by Sex, Race, and
Spanish Origin: 1980

	United States
Demographic Characteristics	
Aggregate population	
Report limited to civilian labor force	1,2
Age	
Report limited to persons 16+ years	1,2
Race - by sex	1,2
White	1,2
Black	1,2
American Indian, Eskimo and Aleut	1,2
Asian and Pacific Islander	1,2
Race not classified	1,2
Spanish Origin	1
Sex	1,2
Social and Economic Characteristics	
Education	
Years of school completed	3,4
by race, by sex	3,4
by Spanish origin/not by Spanish origin, by sex	3
Labor Force	
By race, by sex	1
By Spanish origin/not by Spanish origin, by sex	1
Occupations	
Detailed occupations by race, by sex	1,2
Detailed occupations by Spanish origin, by sex	1

Decennial Year	1980
Census	Twentieth Decennial Census
Volume	Supplementary Report 9
Title	State of Residence in 1975 by State of Residence in 1980
Publication	Department of Commerce, Bureau of the Census Washington, DC: Government Printing Office
Date	1983

Classifications

Supt. of Documents	C 3.223/12:980-S 1-9
Library of Congress	HA 201.1980.B A569x
card	84-602973
Dewey	312.0973
Census designation	PC80-S1-9

Microforms

A.S.I.	ASI 1983 2535-1.9
Pages	10 pages
Maps, illustrations	None
Notes	This report, with but two tables, provides data on migration in the five year period prior to the 1980 census.

1980
Supplementary Report 9   State of Residence in 1975 by State of Residence in 1980

	United States	Regions, Divisions	States
Demographic Characteristics			
Aggregate population			
Limited to persons 5+ years	1	1	1
Age			
Limited to persons 5+ years; no age data			
Social and Economic Characteristics			
Migration/mobility			
Residence in same house in 1975	1	1	1
Residence in different house in 1975			
in the United States	1	1	1
in the same county	1	1	1
in the same state	1	1	1
in a different state	1	1	1
by state	1	1	1
abroad in 1975	1	1	1
in Puerto Rico	1	1	1
in other outlying areas	1	1	1
elsewhere	1	1	1
State immigrants by region of origin	2	2	2
State outmigrants by region of destination	2	2	2
Net migration	2	2	2

Decennial Year	1980
Census	Twentieth Decennial Census
Volume	Supplementary Report 10
Title	Ancestry of the Population by State: 1980
Publication	Department of Commerce, Bureau of the Census Washington, DC: Government Printing Office
Date	1983

Classifications

Supt. of Documents	C 3.223/12:980-S 1-10
Library of Congress	HA 201.1980.B A569x
card	84-602973
Dewey	312.0973
Census designation	PC80-S1-10

Microforms

A.S.I.	ASI 1983 2535-1.10

Pages	84 pages
Maps, illustrations	None
Notes	The 1980 census was the first one in which persons were asked to state their ancestry. This report provides data on over 100 ancestry groups.
	There are four tables, the last of which shows the rank by states for ancestry groups of 100,000 or more.

1980
Supplementary Report 10   Ancestry of the Population by State: 1980

	United States	Regions, Divisions	States
Demographic Characteristics			
Aggregate population	1	1	1
Social and Economic Characteristics			
Nativity			
Ancestry			
persons who reported at least			
one specific ancestry	1,2,3	1,3	1,3
single ancestry	1,3a	1,3a	1,3a
multiple ancestry	1	1	1
by detailed ancestry group	2,3	3	3
single ancestry group	3a	3a	3a
multiple ancestry group	3b	3b	3b
rank of states for ancestry			
groups of 100,000 persons	4	4	4
percent of ancestry group for			
the state	4	4	4

Decennial Year	1980
Census	Twentieth Decennial Census
Volume	Supplementary Report 11
Title	Congressional District Profiles, 98th Congress
Publication	Department of Commerce, Bureau of the Census Washington, DC: Government Printing Office
Date	1983

Classifications

Supt. of Documents	C 3.223/12:980-S1-11
Library of Congress	HA 201.1980.B A569x
card	84-602973
Dewey	312.0973
Census designation	PC80-S1-11

Microforms

A.S.I.	ASI 1983 2535-1.11
Pages	v, 52 pages
Maps, illustrations	One map showing all Congressional Districts
Notes	This report is a national summary of the 1980 series of PHC-4, Congressional Districts of the 98th Congress, in which one report was published for each state. It serves as a good comparison between districts on a variety of demographic and socioeconomic characteristics.

1980
Supplementary Report 11 Congressional District Profiles, 98th
Congress

	United States	States	Congressional Districts
Demographic Characteristics			
Aggregate population	1	1	1
Percent change from 1970	1	1	1
Percent deviation from state average			1
Age			
Median age	1	1	1
Voting age, 18+ years	1	1	1
by race and Spanish origin	1	1	1
Percent 65+ years	1	1	1
Race			
White, Black, other	1	1	1
Spanish origin	1	1	1
Sex	3	3	3
Social and Economic Characteristics			
Education			
School enrollment - Kindergarden through 12th grade	2	2	2
percent in private school	2	2	2
College enrollment	2	2	2
Years of school completed	2	2	2
Employment/unemployment	3	3	3
Class of employer	3	3	3
Percent unemployed	3	3	3
Families	2	2	2
With own children under 18 years	2	2	2
With two or more workers in 1979	2	2	2
With female householder	4	4	4
Farmers			
Percent rural farm	2	2	2

1980
Supplementary Report 11 Congressional District Profiles, 98th Congress

	United States	States	Congressional Districts
Housing			
Number units	4	4	4
Persons per household	4	4	4
Tenure - percent owners, renters	4	4	4
Percent with 1+ persons per room	4	4	4
Income			
Family income	2	2	2
by race and Spanish origin	2	2	2
Household income	2	2	2
Per capita income	2	2	2
Industry	3	3	3
Labor force	3	3	3
Percent women in labor force	3	3	3
Migration/mobility			
Percent born in state of residence	2,3	2,3	2,3
Residence in 1975	2	2	2
Military			
Number in Armed Forces	3	3	3
Veterans	3	3	3
Poverty			
Percent below poverty level by race and Spanish origin	2	2	2

Apportionment, Geography

Apportionment	1	1	1
Percent voting for Congress 1982	1	1	1
Percent voting for winning candidate	1	1	1
Inside/outside metropolitan areas	1	1	1
Urban/rural	1	1	1
Rural farm/nonfarm	2	2	2
percent rural farm	2	2	2

Decennial Year	1980
Census	Twentieth Decennial Census
Volume	Supplementary Report 12
Title	Asian and Pacific Islander Population by State: 1980
Publication	Department of Commerce, Bureau of the Census Washington, DC: Government Printing Office
Date	1983

Classifications

Supt. of Documents	C 3.223/12:980-S1-12
Library of Congress	HA 201.1980.B A569x
card	84-602973
Dewey	312.0973
Census designation	PC80-S1-12

Microforms

A.S.I.	ASI 1984 2535-1.15
Pages	iv, 22 pages
Maps, illustrations	One map in color.
Notes	This report shows over 25 identified racial groups among Asians and Pacific Islanders. Data are given for regions, divisions and states.

1980
Supplementary Report 12 Asian and Pacific Islander Population by
State: 1980

	United States	Regions, Divisions	States
Demographic Characteristics			
Aggregate population	1	1	1
Race			
For all groups categorized see	F		
Asian and Pacific Islanders - each group	1	1	1
Chinese	1	1	1
Filipino	1	1	1
Japanese	1	1	1
Asian Indian	1	1	1
Korean	1	1	1
Vietnamese	1	1	1
Hawaiian	1	1	1
Samoan	1	1	1
Guamanian	1	1	1
other Asian	1	1	1
other Pacific Islanders	1	1	1
Percent of total population	1	1	1
historic from 1910	3	3	3
percent by region and state	3	3	3
Asian population - each group	4	4	4
Asian Indian	4	4	4
Bangladeshi	4	4	4
Burmese	4	4	4
Cambodian (Kampuchean)	4	4	4
Sri Lankan (Ceylonese)	4	4	4
Chinese	4	4	4
Filipino	4	4	4
Hmong	4	4	4
Indonesian	4	4	4
Japanese	4	4	4
Korean	4	4	4
Laotian	4	4	4
Malayan	4	4	4
Okinawan	4	4	4
Pakistani	4	4	4
Thai	4	4	4
Vietnamese	4	4	4
Asian not specified	4	4	4
all other Asian	4	4	4

1980
Supplementary Report 12 Asian and Pacific Islander Population by
State: 1980

	United States	Regions, Divisions	States
Pacific Islander - each group	5	5	5
Polynesian	5	5	5
Hawaiian	5	5	5
Samoan	5	5	5
Tahitian	5	5	5
Tongan	5	5	5
all other	5	5	5
Micronesian	5	5	5
Guamanian	5	5	5
North Mariana Islander	5	5	5
Marshallese	5	5	5
Palauan	5	5	5
all other	5	5	5
Melanesian	5	5	5
Fijian	5	5	5
all other	5	5	5
Pacific Islander not specified	5	5	5

Decennial Year	1980
Census	Twentieth Decennial Census
Volume	Supplementary Report 13
Title	American Indian Areas and Alaska Native Villages: 1980
Publication	Department of Commerce, Bureau of the Census Washington, DC: Government Printing Office
Date	1984

Classifications

Supt. of Documents	C 3.223/12:980-S 1-13
Library of Congress	HA 201.1980.B A569x
card	84-602973
Dewey	312.0973
Census designation	PC80-S1-13

Microforms

A.S.I.	ASI 1984 2535-1.16
Pages	vi, 38 pages
Maps, illustrations	2 maps and one chart in color.
Notes	This report includes corrected data which provides more accurate information on Indian population than Volume I Chapter B.

In addition to the main tables of the report, there are 15 text tables in the introductory pages which should be consulted by anyone needing precise information on Indian and Alaskan population.

1980
Supplementary Report 13 American Indian Areas and Alaska Native
Villages: 1980

	United States	Regns. Divns.	States	Resvtns., Places, Other
Demographic Characteristics				
Aggregate population	1	1	1,4	
Race				
Report limited to American Indians, Eskimos and Aleuts	1	1	1	
percent each of total group	1	1	1	
Number of Indians by place of residence	2	2	2	
Number Indians on each reservation and tribal trust land, percent of all races there	3			3
Indians and others in Oklahoma historic areas			5	
Indians and others in Alaska Native villages				6,7,8
Social and Economic Characteristics				
Housing				
Occupied housing units on Indian reservations and tribal trust lands, Indian or other householder				3
In historic areas of Oklahoma			5	
In Alaska Native villages				6
Households				
American Indian householder or spouse on reservations and tribal trust lands				3
Apportionment, Geography				
American Indian reservations	3,4	3,4	4	3,4
Indians and others living on reservations	3,4	3,4		3,4
Rank by population				9

1980
**Supplementary Report 13 American Indian Areas and Alaska Native
Villages: 1980**

	United States	Reg., Divns.	States	Resvtns., Places, Other
Tribal trust lands	3,4	3,4	3,4	3,4
Indians and others living on				
tribal trust lands	3,4	3,4	3,4	3,4
Historic areas of Oklahoma				
Number and percent Indians			5	5
Alaska Native villages				10
By rank				10
by Eskimo population				11
by Aleut population				12

Decennial Year	1980
Census	Twentieth Decennial Census
Volume	Supplementary Report 14
Title	Population and Land Area of Urbanized Areas for the United States and Puerto Rico: 1980 and 1970
Publication	Department of Commerce, Bureau of the Census Washington, DC: Government Printing Office
Date	1984

Classifications

Supt. of Documents	C 3.223/12:980-S 1-14
Library of Congress	HA 201.1980.B A569x
card	84-602973
Dewey	312.0973
Census designation	PC80-S1-14

Microforms

A.S.I.	ASI 1985 2535-1.17
Pages	iv, 475 pages
Maps, illustrations	Maps of all urbanized areas, alphabetically by state as part of Table 7.
Notes	Information on the 366 urbanized areas in the United States and the 7 in Puerto Rico is provided in this volume. Population data for 1980 and 1970 are given for each component part of each urbanized area, as well as land area in both square miles and square kilometers.
	The concept of "urbanized areas" was developed by the Census Bureau in an effort to provide a better separation of urban and rural population in the vicinity of large cities. An urbanized area consists of one or more central cities and surrounding closely settled territory or urban fringe.

1980
Supplementary Report 14 Population and Land Area of Urbanized Areas
for the United States and Puerto Rico: 1980 and 1970

	United States	Urbanized Areas	Component Parts
Demographic Characteristics			
Aggregate population	3	1,2,7	7
Urbanized areas		1,2,7	
historic from 1970		7	7
by rank			2
Component parts			7
Central cities			1,7
by inside/outside			4
Extended cities			6
Apportionment, Geography			
Density		1	1
Land area in miles and kilometers		1	1
of extended cities			6
By size of place	5		
Urbanized areas		1	
Inside/outside central cities			1
By size of place	3		
Historic for 1970	3		

Decennial Year	1980
Census	Twentieth Decennial Census
Volume	Supplementary Report 15
Title	Detailed Occupation of the Experienced Civilian Labor Force by Sex for the United States and Regions: 1980 and 1970
Publication	Department of Commerce, Bureau of the Census Washington, DC: Government Printing Office
Date	1984

Classifications

Supt. of Documents	C 3.223/12:980-S 1-15
Library of Congress	HA 201.1980.B A569x
card	84-602973
Dewey	312.0973
Census designation	PC80-S1-15

Microforms

A.S.I.	ASI 1984 2535-1.12

Pages	51 pages
Maps, illustrations	One map of Census Regions and Divisions.
Note	The 1980 data in this report were derived from the computer file titled "1980 Census EEO Special File" which was produced to meet the needs of employers in planning Equal Employment Opportunity/Affirmative Action efforts. The 1970 data were derived from the 1970 census "Sixth-Count" data file.

The occupational classification system used in the 1980 Census is based on the Standard Occupational Classification system.

Data are provided for the United States as a whole and for four regions: West, North Central, Northeast and South.

1980
**Supplementary Report 15 Detailed Occupation of the Experienced
Civilian Labor Force by Sex for the United States and Regions:
1980 and 1970**

	United States	Regions
Note: There is a single table in this report.		
Demographic Characteristics		
Age Limited to persons 16+ years; no age data.		
Sex All tables are by sex	x	x
Social and Economic Characteristics		

Labor force
  This report is limited to persons in
    the experienced civilian labor force.
	x	x

Occupations
  Detailed occupations by sex
  Historic from 1970
	x
	x
		x
		x

Decennial Year	1980
Census	Twentieth Decennial Census
Volume	Supplementary Report 16
Title	Residence in 1975 for States by Age, Sex, Race, and Spanish Origin
Publication	Department of Commerce, Bureau of the Census Washington, DC: Government Printing Office
Date	1984
Classifications	
Supt. of Documents	C 3.223/12:980-S 1-16
Library of Congress	HA 201.1980.B A569x
card	84-602973
Dewey	312.0973
Census designation	PC80-S1-16
Microforms	
A.S.I.	ASI 1984 2535-1.13
Pages	v, 336 pages
Maps, illustrations	None
Notes	This report provides information on mobility during the 1975-1980 period. Answers to the April 1, 1975, question on residence were compared with residence at the time of the 1980 enumeration and classified by demographic characteristics. Additional data are given for the number of persons in the military or attending college in 1975 and 1980.

1980
Supplementary Report 16   Residence in 1975 for States by Age, Sex, Race, and Spanish Origin

	United States	Regions	States

Note: There is a single table in this report.

<u>Demographic Characteristics</u>

	United States	Regions	States
Aggregate population			
Limited to persons 5+ years	x	x	x
Age - groups			
Persons 5+ years, by sex	x	x	x
Persons 16+ years	x	x	x
Persons 21+ years	x	x	x
Race			
White	x	x	x
Black	x	x	x
American Indian, Eskimo, Aleut	x	x	x
Asian and Pacific Islander	x	x	x
Other	x	x	x
Spanish origin	x	x	x
Sex	x	x	x

<u>Social and Economic Characteristics</u>

	United States	Regions	States
Education			
Persons attending college in 1980, 1975	x	x	x
Migration/mobility			
By age, race, sex and Spanish origin	x	x	x
Residence in 1975 - same house	x	x	x
Residence in 1975 - different house	x	x	x
same/different county	x	x	x
same/different state	x	x	x
different state, by region	x	x	x
abroad	x	x	x
Military			
In armed forces 1980, 1975	x	x	x

Decennial Year	1980
Census	Twentieth Decennial Census
Volume	Supplementary Report 17
Title	Gross Migration for Counties: 1975 to 1980
Publication	Department of Commerce, Bureau of the Census Washington, DC: Government Printing Office
Date	1984

Classifications

Supt. of Documents	C 3.223/12:980-S 1-17
Library of Congress	HA 201.1980.B A569x
card	84-602973
Dewey	312.0973
Census designation	PC80-S1-17

Microforms

A.S.I.	ASI 1984 2535-1.14
Pages	246 pages
Maps, illustrations	None
Notes	In this report, data on migration between 1975 and 1980 are provided by state and county. Sex, and race and Spanish origin of migrants is shown. Additional tables provide specific data for New York City.

1980
Supplementary Report 17 Gross Migration for Counties: 1975 to 1980

	State	Counties
Demographic Characteristics		
Aggregate population	x	x
Age	x	x
Race	x	x
Spanish origin	x	x
Sex	x	x
Social and Economic Characteristics		
Education		
Attending college 1975 or 1980	x	x
Migration/mobility	x	x
In-migrants 1975-1980	x	x
Out-migrants 1975-1980	x	x
Net migrants 1975-1980	x	x
Military/veterans		
In armed forces 1975 or 1980	x	x
Apportionment, Geography		
New York City		
In-migrants 1975-1980		x
Out-migrants 1975-1980		x
Net migrants 1975-1980		x

Decennial Year	1980
Census	Twentieth Decennial Census
Volume	Supplementary Report 18
Title	Metropolitan Statistical Areas (as defined by the Office of Management and Budget in 1983)
Publication	Department of Commerce, Bureau of the Census Washington, DC: Government Printing Office
Date	1985

Classifications

Supt. of Documents	C 3.223/12:980-S1-18
Library of Congress	HA 201.1980.B A569x
card	84-602973
Dewey	312.0973
Census designation	PC80-S1-18

Microforms

A.S.I.	ASI 1985 2535-1.18
Pages	188 pages
Maps, illustrations	None
Notes	The title of this report calls attention to the fact that it is not the Census Bureau, but the Office of Management and Budget, which determines Metropolitan Statistical Areas and sets their boundaries. This report includes areas designated as late as 1983.
	There are numerous useful text tables and appendix tables as well as the 8 detailed tables in this report. It also includes an alphabetical list of Metropolitan Statistical Areas and another of central cities.

1980
Supplementary Report 18 Metropolitan Statistical Areas (as defined by the Office of Management and Budget in 1983)

	Regns., Divns, States	Consol. MSA's, Primary MSA's	Component Parts
Demographic Characteristics			
Aggregate population	x	x	x
Historic from 1970	x	x	x
Rank	x	x	x
Race	x	x	x
Spanish origin	x	x	x
Social and Economic Characteristics			
Households	x	x	x
Historic from 1970	x	x	x
Persons per household	x	x	x
Group quarters	x	x	x
Housing			
Number units	x	x	x
Apportionment, Geography			
Density	x	x	x
Inside/outside central cities			x

Decennial Year	1980
Census	Twentieth Decennial Census
Volume	Supplementary Report 19
Title	Rural and Farm Population by Current (1980) and Previous (1970) Farm Definitions, for States and Counties: 1980
Publication	Department of Commerce, Bureau of the Census Washington, DC: Government Printing Office
Date	1985

Classifications

Supt. of Documents	C 3.223/12:980-S 1-19
Library of Congress	HA 201.1980.B A569x
card	84-602973
Dewey	312.0973
Census designation	PC80-S1-19

Microforms

A.S.I.	ASI 1985 2535-1.19
Pages	22 pages
Maps, illustrations	None
Notes	There is a single table in this report. In 4 separate columns, it provides a count of the total population for each state and county. It sets out the rural population, and the population on farms in 1980 by the 1980 farm definition and by the 1970 definition.

1980
Supplementary Report 19   Rural and Farm Population by Current (1980)
and Previous (1970) Farm Definitions, for States and Counties: 1980

	United States	States	Counties
Demographic Characteristics			
Aggregate population	x	x	x
Social and Economic Characteristics			
Farmers, farms			
Farm population, 1980*	x	x	x
Farm population, 1980 by 1970 definition			
of farms	x	x	x
Apportionment, Geography			
Rural	x	x	x

*The 1980 definition of a farm established agricultural sales of
$1,000 as a minimum standard. The 1970 and 1960 Census definitions
had set $50 of agricultural sales as the standard. This report is
restricted to the 1980 population and shows that population as farm
population under the 1980 and 1970 definitions.

Decennial Year	1980
Census	Twentieth Decennial Census
Volume	Supplementary Report 20
Title	Selected Characteristics of Persons with a Work Disability by State: 1980
Publication	Department of Commerce, Bureau of the Census Washington, DC: Government Printing Office
Date	1985

Classifications

Supt. of Documents	C 3.223/12:980-S1-20
Library of Congress	HA 201.1980.B A569x
card	84-602973
Dewey	312.0973
Census designation	PC80-S1-20

Microforms

A.S.I.	ASI 1985 2535-1.20
Pages	137 Pages
Maps, illustrations	None
Notes	In the 1980 census the question on disability was limited to persons 15+ plus years. This report is limited to persons 16 to 64 years. They were asked whether they had a disability which limited the amount or kind of work they could do and whether or not they were prevented from working at all. A physical or mental health condition of 6 months determined disability. In this report data are presented by Census Regions, Divisions and states.

1980
Supplementary Report 20 Selected Characteristics of Persons with a
Work Disability by State: 1980

	United States	Regions	States
Demographic Characteristics			
Age			
Report limited to persons 16-64 years	x	x	x
Race	x	x	x
Spanish origin	x	x	x
Sex	x	x	x
Social and Economic Characteristics			
Disability			
Prevented from working	x	x	x
Education			
Years of school completed	x	x	x
Employment/unemployment			
Worked in 1979 50-52 weeks	x	x	x
Class of employer	x	x	x
Mean number weeks of unemployment 1979	x	x	x
Income	x	x	x
Labor force	x	x	x
Occupation	x	x	x
Poverty level	x	x	x
Apportionment, Geography			
Inside/outside metropolitan areas	x	x	x
Inside/outside central cities	x	x	x

Decennial Year	1980
Census	Twentieth Decennial Census
Volume	Advance Reports
Title	Final Population and Housing Unit Counts
Publication	Department of Commerce, Bureau of the Census Washington, DC: Government Printing Office
Date	1981

Classifications

Supt. of Documents	C3.223/19:980/1-52
Library of Congress	HA201.1980 A5427
Dewey	312.0973
Census designation	PC80-C-1-52
Microforms	None
Pages	Vary
Maps, illustrations	None
Notes	Issued in paper, printed in brown, these reports made available the first final counts of population resulting from the 1980 enumeration. There was one report issued for each state, one for the District of Columbia, and one summary for the United States.

These reports contained data for Congressional Districts of the 96th Congress. Such data did not appear in any other 1980 Census publication. |

1980
Advance Reports Final Population and Housing Unit Counts

	The State	Congnl. Dists.	Counties, Subdvns.	Places
Demographic Characteristics				
Aggregate population	1	3	1	1,2
Historic from 1970, change	1	3	1	1,2
Race	1	3	1	1,2
White	1	3	1	1,2
Black	1	3	1	1,2
American Indian, Eskimo, Aleut	1	3	1	1,2
Asian and Pacific Islander	1	3	1	1,2
Other	1	3	1	1,2
Spanish origin	1	3	1	1,2
Social and Economic Characteristics				
Housing - number units	1	3	1	1,2

* County subdivisions include Minor Civil Divisions, which are the
  primary divisions of counties established under state law in 29
  states, Census County Divisions in 20 states and Census Subareas in
  Alaska.

Table 1 includes counts for all Minor Civil Divisions. Table 2 includes counts for all places incorporated under their state laws
listed alphabetically by name of place.

Decennial Year	1980
Census	Twentieth Decennial Census
Volume	Final Reports
Title	1980 Census of Population and Housing Census Tracts
Publication	Department of Commerce, Bureau of the Census Washington, DC: Government Printing Office
Date	1984 and 1985

Classifications

Supt. of Documents	C 3.223/11:980/1-9, 11-53, 58-380
Library of Congress	HA 201.1980.h nos.
card	81-607944
Dewey	312.0973
Census designation	PHC80-2-1-9, 11-53, 58-380

Microforms

A.S.I.	ASI 1984 and 1985 2551-2.1 through 2551-2.53, 2551-2.58 through 2551-2.380
Pages	Vary
Maps, illustrations	Each SMSA census tract report volume is accompanied by an envelope containing a map of the Standard Metropolitan Statistical Area showing its census tract boundaries. Each state report volume has accompanying maps for each of the tracted areas outside SMSAs.
Notes	These reports include data from both the population and the housing inquiries of the 1980 census. There are reports for each SMSA, for each state with tracted areas outside SMSAs, for Puerto Rico, and a U.S. summary.

	SMSA	Component Parts	Tracts
Demographic Characteristics			
Aggregate population	P1	P1	P1
Age	P6	P6	P6
Race	P1,7	P1,7	P1,7
White	P2,12,13	P2,12,13	P2,12,13
Black	P3,14,15	P3,14,15	P3,14,15
American Indian, Eskimo, Aleut	P4,16,17	P4,16,17	P4,16,17
Asian and Pacific Islander	P5,18,19	P5,18,19	P5,18,19
Spanish origin	P6,7,20, 21	P6,7,20, 21	P6,7,20, 21
Mexican, Puerto Rican, Cuban, other Spanish	P7	P7	P7
Sex	P1-6	P1-6	P1-6
Marital status	P1-6	P1-6	P1-6
Social and Economic Characteristics			
Disabilities	P10,12,14, 16,18,20	P10,12,14, 16,18,20	P10,12,14, 16,18,20
Education			
School enrollment	P9,12,14, 16,18,20	P9,12,14, 16,18,20	P9,12,14, 16,18,20
private schools	P9		
persons 16-19 not in school	P10		
Years of school completed	P9,12,14, 16,18,20	P9,12,14, 16,18,20	P9,12,14, 16,18,20
Employment/unemployment	P10,12,14, 16,18,20	P10,12,14, 16,18,20	P10,12,14, 16,18,20
Place of work, re SMSA	P9		
Families	P1-6	P1-6	P1-6
Number workers in family	P10		
Fertility	P9,12,14, 16,18,20	P9,12,14, 16,18,20	P9,12,14, 16,18,20

1980
Final Reports   1980 Census of Population and Housing   Census Tracts

	SMSA	Component Parts	Tracts
Households	P1-6,11	P1-6,11	P1-6,11
Persons living alone	P1-6	P1-6	P1-6
Persons 65+ years	P1-6	P1-6	P1-6
Group quarters	P1-6	P1-6	P1-6
Housing	H1,7,8	H1,7,8	H1,7,8
Income	P11,13,15, 17,19,21	P11,13,15, 17,19,21	P11,13,15, 17,19,21
By type	P11		
By household tenure	P11		
Industry	P10	P10	P10
Institutional population	P1-6	P1-6	P1-6
Labor force	P10,12,14, 16,18,20	P10,12,14, 16,18,20	P10,12,14, 16,18,20
Language			
Speaks other than English at home; speaks English not well or not at all	P9,12,14, 16,18,20	P9,12,14, 16,18,20	P9,12,14, 16,18,20
Migration/mobility	P9		
Residence in 1975	P9,12,14, 16,18,20	P9,12,14, 16,18,20	P9,12,14, 16,18,20
Nativity	P9,12,14, 16,18,20	P9,12,14, 16,18,20	P9,12,14, 16,18,20
Occupations	P10,13,15, 17,19,21	P10,13,15, 17,19,21	P10,13,15, 17,19,21
Poverty	P11,13,15, 17,19,21	P11,13,15, 17,19,21	P11,13,15, 17,19,21
Transportation			
Journey to work	P9,12,14, 16,18,20	P9,12,14, 16,18,20	P9,12,14, 16,18,20
Travel time	P9,12,14, 16,18,20	P9,12,14, 16,18,20	P9,12,14, 16,18,20

Decennial Year	1980
Census	Twentieth Decennial Census
Volume	Final Reports
Title	1980 Census of Population and Housing Summary Characteristics for Governmental Units and Standard Metropolitan Statistical Areas
Publication	Department of Commerce, Bureau of the Census Washington, DC: Government Printing Office
Date	1982 and 1983

Classifications

Supt. of Documents	C 3.223/23:980/2-53
Library of Congress	HA 201.1980i
card	81-607959
Dewey	312.0973
Census designation	PHC80-33-2-53

Microforms

A.S.I.	ASI 1982 and 1983 2551-3.2 through 2551-3.53

Pages	Vary
Maps, illustrations	None
Notes	These 52 reports, one for each state, one for the District of Columbia, and one for Puerto Rico, are among the most useful of the 1980 census publications. They provide basic demographic and socioeconomic data for each state, SMSA, county and place.

1980
Final Reports 1980 Census of Population and Housing
Summary Characteristics for Governmental Units and Standard
Metropolitan Statistical Areas

	State	SMSAs	Counties	Places
Demographic Characteristics				
Aggregate population	1	1	1	1
Noninstitutional population	4	4	4	4
Age	1,3	1,3	1,3	1,3
Race	1	1	1	1
Spanish origin	1	1	1	1
Sex	1	1	1	1
Social and Economic Characteristics				
Disabilities				
Work disability	4	4	4	4
Education				
School enrollment	3	3	3	3
Percent high school graduates	3	3	3	3
Employment/unemployment	3	3	3	3
Percent unemployed	3	3	3	3
Families	1	1	1	1
Households	1	1	1	1
Persons per household	1	1	1	1
Housing	2	2	2	2
Group quarters	1	1	1	1
Income				
For families, households	4	4	4	4
Labor force	3,4	3,4	3,4	3,4

1980
Final Reports 1980 Census of Population and Housing
Summary Characteristics for Governmental Units and Standard
Metropolitan Statistical Areas

	State	SMSAs	Counties	Places
Language				
Speak language other than English at home	3	3	3	3
Speak English not well/not at all	3	3	3	3
Migration/mobility				
Residence in other state in 1975	3	3	3	3
Moved into unit after 1-1-79	5	5	5	5
Poverty	4	4	4	4
By age	4	4	4	4
Status of families with children	4	4	4	4
Transportation				
Means of transportation to work	3	3	3	3
Percent in car pools	3	3	3	3
One or more vehicles at address	5	5	5	5

Decennial Year	1980
Census	Twentieth Decennial Census
Volume	Final Reports
Title	1980 Census of Population and Housing Congressional Districts of the 98th, 99th and 100th Congresses
Publication	Department of Commerce, Bureau of the Census Washington, DC: Government Printing Office
Date	1983, 1985 and 1987

Classifications

Supt. of Documents	C 3.223/20:980/2 through /52 (98th Congress)
Supt. of Documents	C 3.223/20:980/2/2 through /52/2 (99th, 100th)
Library of Congress	HA 201.1980x
card	84-602876
Dewey	312.0973
Census designation	PHC80-4-2-52 (state numbers), PHC80-4-2/2-52/2

Microforms

A.S.I.	ASI 1983 and 1985 2551-4.2 through 2551-4.52
Pages	Vary
Maps, illustrations	Map of state with Congressional Districts and additional maps showing details.
Notes	Data in these reports came from the 1980 Census. For most states the data are based on Congressional Districts of the 98th Congress, elected in November 1972. For nine states which redistricted later, the reports show data for 99th Congress Districts. These include California, Hawaii, Louisiana, Mississippi, Montana, New Jersey, New York, Texas and Washington. There are reports for a few states for the 100th Congress. Corresponding data for the 92d, 93d and 94th Congresses are available in the Congressional District Data series. 97th Congress data are available on microfiche Summary Tape Files 1A and 3A.

1980
Final Reports 1980 Census of Population and Housing Congressional
Districts of the 98th, 99th and 100th Congresses

	State	Congres. Districts	Counties	Places
Demographic Characteristics				
Aggregate population	1	1	2	2
Year-round population	2	2	2	2
Age	1,2,7	1,2,7	2	2
Voting age - persons 18+ years	1,2	1,2	2	2
Race	1,7	1,7		
White	1	1		
Black	1,2	1,2	2	2
American Indian, Eskimo, Aleut	1	1		
Asian and Pacific Islander	1	1		
Other	1	1		
Spanish origin	1,2,7	1,2,7	2	2
Sex	1,5,7	1,5,7		
Marital status	3	3		
Social and Economic Characteristics				
Disabilities				
Work disability	4	4		
Inability to use public transportation	4	4		
Education				
School enrollment	4	4		
Years of school completed	4,7	4,7		
Employment/unemployment	5,7	5,7		
Class of employer	5	5		
Families	1-3,7	1-3,7	2	2
Female head, no husband present	2,3,7	2,3,7	2	2
No workers in family	5	5		
Farmers/farms	3	3		

1980
Final Reports 1980 Census of Population and Housing Congressional Districts of the 98th, 99th and 100th Congresses

	State	Congres. Districts	Counties	Places
Fertility				
Women 15-44, children ever born	3	3		
Households	1-3	1-3		
Group quarters	1,3	1,3		
Nonfamily households	3	3		
Housing	1,2, 8-11	1,2, 8-11	2	2
Income	6,7	6,7		
Industry	5	5		
Institutional population	1,3	1,3		
Labor force	5,7	5,7		
Language				
Language spoken at home	4	4		
Ability to speak English	4	4		
Migration/mobility	4,8	4,8		
Residence in 1975	4	4		
Abroad in 1975	4	4		
Native born, place of birth	4	4		
Military/veterans				
Veteran status	4	4		
Percent males 16+ years, veterans	4	4		
Nativity				
General nativity	4	4		
Ancestry	3	3		
Occupations	5	5		
Poverty	6,7	6,7		
Transportation				
Travel to work	4	4		
Number persons per vehicle	4	4		

1980
Final Reports 1980 Census of Population and Housing Congressional Districts of the 98th, 99th and 100th Congresses

	State	Congres. Districts	Counties	Places
Apportionment, Geography				
Apportionment				
Number Congressional Districts	1	1-11	2	2
Density	1	1		
Urban/rural				
Urban	1,3	1,3		
inside/outside urbanized				
areas	3	3		
Rural	3	3		
farm	3	3		

NOTES ON OTHER 1980 CENSUS PUBLICATIONS
WITH POPULATION INFORMATION

VOLUME	TITLE

Preliminary Reports

Preliminary Population and Housing Unit Counts

This set of reports for each state, and with a U.S. summary, was the first to be issued with population and housing unit counts. It includes counts for the state, counties, county subdivisions, incorporated places, Standard Metropolitan Areas, and Congressional Districts, and provides comparative data for 1970. Though superseded by the Advance Reports, which have final counts, these reports are very useful succinct documents.

C 3.223/18:980-P1-52
PHC80-P1-52

Final Reports

Block Statistics

This group of 375 reports was published in microfiche only, though accompanied by maps printed on paper. The reports were published for all urbanized areas and other selected areas, and include data on both population and housing.

C 3.224/5:(maps)
PHC80-1
LC 81-607960
A.S.I. 1983 2551-1.1 through 2551-1.380

Supplementary Reports

These Supplementary Reports are those of the 1980 Census of Population and Housing, in contrast to those of the 1980 Census of Population.

Advance Estimates of Social, Economic, and Housing Characteristics

This is a very useful series, with one report for each state, for quick reference on basic demographic and socioeconomic data for states and cities of 25,000.

C 3.223/21-2:980-S2-2-52
PHC80-S2-2-52
LC 82-600136
A.S.I. 1982 and 1983 2557-2.2 through 2557-2.52

Indexes

Alphabetical Index of Industries and Occupations

This index is similar to those published for
earlier censuses. The introductory pages include
both the industrial and the occupational classification systems, and are followed in the text by
an alphabetical listing of industries and of occupations.

C 3.223/22:980-R3
Final edition 1982   xviii, I 1-189, O 1-263 pages
LC 80-18360/r834

Classified Index of Industries and Occupations

This volume is a companion to the one above. It
lists industries and occupations by order of their
census classifications.

C 3.223/22:980-R4
Final edition 1982   xciii, I 1-114, O 1-161 pages
LC 83-601032

Geographical Identification Code Scheme

This volume lists all Census Regions and Divisions, states and state equivalents, Standard
Metropolitan Statistical Areas, urbanized areas,
American Indian reservations and Alaska Native
villages, and then, by state, all counties and
county subdivisions and places, together with
various code designations.

C 3.223/22:980-R5
664 pages
82-600298

**Summary
Tape Files**

These files, published only on microfiche, are outside the scope of this guide which is limited to census printed volumes. However, attention should be called to this valuable data.

Summary Tape Files 1 and 2 include complete count data, and Summary Tape Files 3, 4 and 5 include sample estimate data. There is also another group of subject report tapes. Information on these files is available from the Data Users Service of the Census Bureau and from the State Affiliates. Very specific data are available down to the Census Tract and Enumeration District level.

TERMINOLOGY USED IN THIS VOLUME

The following list of terms is an effort to relate the concepts used through the four decennial censuses covered by this guide, and to give some historical perspective on their census use. The best source for the meaning of census terminology is, however, the census itself. No term used in the census goes undefined in its volumes. It is there that anyone should look when a precise definition is required. Insofar as possible, the terminology below is reproduced but abbreviated from the definitions in the original census volumes.

Age. Information on the age of the population has been collected since the First Census in 1790. It was continued through the 1950-1980 Censuses as a complete count item: asked of every person. Age is based on the number of complete years of life as of April 1st of the decennial year. Data on single years of age can be found in at least one volume of each census, although most age data is given for groups of ages. Many tables show median age.

In 1960, for the first time, there was a question on the date of birth. This was based on an effort to reduce "age-heaping," in which overstatement of ages had occurred for ages ending in "0" or "5" and, consequently, understatement of other ages. It should be noted that older ages may also be overstated. Prior to 1940, the Census had published a separate category of persons of unknown age. Since 1940, however, it has assigned the age of persons whose age was not reported according to statistical allocation methods. Any reader needing more precise information should consult the introductory or appendix pages of the appropriate volume.

Aggregate population. Total population.

Alaska Native villages. These are villages of tribes or other groups of Alaska Natives with 25 or more persons, as defined in Public Law 92-203.

Ancestry. Information on ancestry in this volume can be found under the term nativity. It should be noted here, however, that in 1980, one of the sample questions was on the person's ancestry. This question was in place of one on the place of birth of parents which had been used in 1970.

Apportionment. Article I, Section 2 of the United States Constitution states that "Representatives and direct taxes shall be apportioned among the several States which may be included within this

Union, according to their respective numbers. . . .The actual enumeration shall be made within three years after the first meeting of the Congress of the United States, and within every subsequent term of ten years, in such manner as they shall by law direct. . ." This is the basis for the census. The results of the decennial enumeration provide a count for determining the number of representatives for each state, which is generally referred to as apportionment of the seats in the House of Representatives among the states. For this reason, the first publication resulting from a decennial census is the enumeration of the population by states, and the first chapter of the published volumes is entitled "Number of Inhabitants." This provides for the determination of the number of seats for each state in the House of Representatives. After this is done, the legislature or other designated body in each state establishes Congressional Districts in time to provide for primary and general elections in the year ending in "2."

Census County Divisions. These area boundaries were developed by the Census Bureau for 1950 in order to establish areas for statistical data where there were no legally established boundaries. Based on physical features, by 1980 they were used for 20 states.

Census Designated Places. These are areas of closely settled population which have no incorporated boundaries.

Census Geographic Divisions. These are 9 groups of contiguous states established by the Census Bureau in order to provide summary data at an intermediate level. They are in turn grouped into Census Regions. A map showing Geographic Divisions and Regions appears opposite page 1.

Census Regions. These are four large groupings of states: West, South, North Central and Northeast. Each contains two Census Geographic Divisions except the South, which contains three. A map showing these areas appears opposite page 1.

Census Tracts. These are small areas of 3,000 to 6,000 population, developed in cooperation with local authorities to provide statistical data on a small scale. First established for 8 cities in 1910, they have now been developed for virtually all urban areas. Based on physical boundaries such as streets, streams and railroad tracks, rather than on political boundaries, they are intended to remain stable so that population data can be compared from one census to another.

Center of population. Throughout most of its history, the Census has calculated the movement of population by designating a center of population - a point where a north-south line crosses an east-west line, with one half the population on each side. The center of population has generally moved west and somewhat south. Maps published in each census showing the center of population provide a dramatic picture of the movement of population over the 200 years of the nation's history.

Citizenship. Oddly enough, the Census has not always inquired as to citizenship. In 1950, 1970 and 1980, there were inquiries as to where a person was born, and data on citizenship is included in census reports for those years. No data on citizenship is published in the 1960 volumes except for Americans abroad who used a separate schedule.

Class of employer, class of worker. The term class of worker is used through the published reports of these four censuses to mean the category of employer or source of employment: private employer, government employer, self-employed or unpaid family worker. Government workers include those in the armed forces, and unpaid family workers include those who work without pay, such as on a farm or in a business owned by one to whom they are related by blood or marriage, such as spouse or children. About one quarter of those in this category are farm workers. In this volume, class of worker is used as being more properly descriptive, and data are found in tables listed under employment/unemployment.

Color. The Census has historically used the term color in place of race, and sometimes ethnic group. Frequently, tables in which the word color is used divide the population enumerated into two categories: White and nonwhite. In that case, nonwhite includes all races other than White. In this guide, the term race is used regardless of how many categories are used in the tables, and the term color is not used at all.

Complete count. This term is used to refer to enumeration items which were asked of the entire population, as opposed to only a sample portion. Beginning with 1940, the Census began to use advanced sampling procedures for the major portion of items on its questionnaire. Those items were asked of only a portion of the population. Items which have been included in the complete count for the years 1950 through 1980 are age, race, sex, marital status, and relation to the head of the household or, in 1980, to the first person named for the household. Descriptive pages included in each census explain which questions are sample questions and how the sample was drawn.

The 1950 schedule also included a <u>complete count</u> item on place of birth and, if foreign born, whether naturalized. The 1980 schedule had a <u>complete count</u> question, "Is this person of Spanish/Hispanic origin or descent?"

<u>Congressional District</u>. This is an area within a state from which a Representative in Congress is elected. Such districts are determined in each state after the apportionment following each census.

<u>Demographic characteristics</u>. These characteristics of the population include age, sex, race and marital status. In this guide, wherever Spanish surname or Spanish origin are shown, these are included among <u>demographic characteristics</u>.

<u>Density</u>. Population per land area, usually stated as persons per square mile.

<u>Disabilities</u>. Although there were questions as to disabilities in the last decades of the nineteenth century, and numerous volumes with reports of the results published, questions in this area declined so that by 1940 no question was included in the enumeration. The next two censuses, 1950 and 1960, likewise had no question on the subject.

The 1970 schedule included sample questions "Does this person have a health or physical condition which limits the kind or amount of work he can do at a job?" and "Does his health or physical condition keep him from holding any job at all?" And if so, "How long has he been limited in his ability to work?" There was no question as to the type of disability, nor was the question used for school age children, only for those old enough to work. Similarly, in 1980, the questions were, "Does this person have a physical, mental, or other health condition which has lasted for 6 or more months and which a) limits the kind or amount of work this person can do at a job, b) prevents this person from working at a job, or c) limits or prevents this person from using public transportation?" The appendices in both censuses refer to "work disability." In view of the legislation passed in the 1970's and 1980's on education of, services for, and nondiscrimination against the handicapped, it was indeed unfortunate that the questions were limited to older persons. In 1970, they were asked of those 14 to 64 years, and answers were published for those 16 to 64.

<u>Earnings</u>. Wage and salary income and proceeds from self-employment. This is a category within the general term income, but most census tables do not make the distinction.

Economic Subregion. These are groups of State Economic Areas; both
of these terms were used in 1950 and 1960. There were 121 Economic
Subregions and 509 State Economic Areas in 1960. Although the latter were confined within state boundaries, the larger Subregions
crossed state lines.

Education. Although questions on literacy had dominated the questionnaires in the nineteenth century, accompanied by a question on
school attendance, they were dropped in favor of questions on school
attendance and years of school completed, in the twentieth century,
with considerable data published for the years 1950-1980. A standard
figure of median years of school completed by persons 25 years and
over is provided in each census. In a few instances data are also
available for job or other vocational training.

Employment/Unemployment. Each decennial census since 1820 has had
a question on employment, and the 1950-1980 Censuses followed that
tradition. The 1950 and 1960 Censuses inquired as to employment of
those persons 14 and over, and the 1970 and 1980 Censuses of those
16 and over, although some data for those 15 and 16 were also published. Employment and unemployment have quite technical meanings
in census terminology, and those needing precise data should be sure
to consult the introductory or appendix sections of the appropriate
volumes.

Generally, those employed are those who were at work during the week
the census was taken, including those who had jobs but were not at
work (excluding those on layoffs). Those unemployed were those
not at work, those without jobs, those on layoff, and those looking
for work and available to accept a job. Those who worked 15 hours or
more on a family farm or other enterprise but were unpaid, were considered employed. The terms employment and unemployment are used
in connection with the term labor force. Those needing precise data
should consult the introductory or appendix sections of the appropriate volumes for a proper interpretation of the data.

Families. This term has been used since the earliest decennial censuses, but in more recent censuses it must be considered in relation
to data on households. Generally a family has consisted of a head
of household and those living in the same household who are related
by blood, marriage or adoption. The 1960 Census used the term primary family for such a group, and the term secondary family for
those related to each other but not to the household family such as
lodgers and resident employees. The latter group had become so small
by 1960 that it was not used in 1970, and those who might have been
included were relegated to the term secondary individuals. In 1970
data were published on married couples and subfamilies (married couples or single persons with one or more single children living in a

household and related to, but not including, the head of the household or his wife).

Farmers, farms. Most of the data on farmers appears in the various tables on occupations and industries. However, where there are occasional references to farmers elsewhere in the population volumes, they are shown here. By 1950, the Census of Agriculture had become a separate census, taken apart from the Census of Population, and it was later published for nondecennial years. Those needing data on farmers will find more in the agricultural volumes.

Data on rural population are divided into two groups, rural-farm, for those persons living on farms, and rural non-farm for all other persons in rural areas.

Fertility. A term which refers to the number of children ever born to a woman. The fertility rate is the number of children born per 1,000 women of childbearing age. Prior to 1980, the question on fertility was asked of ever-married women and of women who completed self-administered questionnaires. In 1980, the question was asked of all females of 15 years or more.

Foreign stock. A term used in 1970 to refer to the foreign born and the native population of foreign or mixed parentage.

Geography. In an effort to enumerate the population, it has been necessary for the Census throughout its history to devote considerable attention to this discipline. It is essential to establish boundaries of states, counties, minor civil divisions and other census-determined areas before the population is enumerated. A great deal of definitive geographical data is therefore included in census volumes. The Bureau publishes maps to show the boundary of each entity referred to in census reports. Maps are frequently included with published reports.

Group quarters. In 1970 and 1980 census reports used this term to refer to persons not living in households. These include inmates of all types of institutions, such as hospitals, group homes, prisons, college dormitories, armed forces barracks, and on military or naval ships. Also included are persons in shelters, living in railroad stations, and, sadly, the homeless. The Census Bureau made a major effort in 1980 to reach this population, which had presumably been undercounted in previous decennial censuses.

<u>Head of household</u>. A term used up through the 1970 census for one person in each <u>household</u>: the one appearing first on the enumeration form. In 1980, the one adult who was listed first on the questionnaire was designated <u>householder</u>.

<u>Household</u>. Although the strict definition of the term has varied slightly over the various decades, generally the term has meant the persons who inhabit a single dwelling unit, living and eating as a separate group, with separate access from outside or from a hallway. <u>Persons per household</u> is determined by dividing the number of <u>households</u> by the number of persons inhabiting them. <u>Households</u> are distinguished from <u>families</u> in modern census reports.

<u>Housing</u>. The Census has traditionally collected information on the housing of the population. However, in 1940 for the first time, the Census of Housing was separated from the Census of Population. Since then little information on <u>housing</u> has been published in the latter. There are, however, a few census publications which include both, such as <u>Census Tract Reports</u> and where that occurs, reference is made in this guide.

<u>Immigration</u>. Information on this question has not always been included in the population questionnaire and was not asked in 1950 or 1960. It was, however, asked in 1970 and 1980 of those who were foreign born. "Born abroad of American parents" was the term used for those who were born American citizens. <u>Immigration</u> data are thus available for 1970 and 1980 in census volumes, as it had been from 1890 through 1930. Data on <u>immigration</u> can of course be obtained from other U.S. sources, such as annual reports of the Bureau of Immigration, a section of the Justice Department. It should be noted that one of the monographs published privately in connection with the 1950 Census was titled <u>Immigrants and Their Children</u>. (See note at the end of the 1950 chapter.)

<u>Income</u>. Data on <u>income</u> generally refer to that from the prior year, i.e. the year ending in "9." Data on this subject were collected in each of the years 1950 through 1980, although there are some differences in definitions. The introductions or appendices should be consulted for exact interpretations. Generally included are wages and salaries, farm and nonfarm self-employment monies, interest and dividends, social security and pensions, and welfare payments. Data in most published reports are provided for <u>household income</u> and <u>family income</u>, often with a median or mean shown, and also <u>per capita income</u>, which is based on the total population divided by the total <u>income</u> for the geographical entity.

<u>Indian Reservation</u>. Areas set aside by treaty, statute, executive
or court order for American Indians. The boundaries have been determined by the Bureau of Indian Affairs and appropriate state govern-
ments.

<u>Indians</u>. American <u>Indians</u> are counted as a separate race in the
modern censuses. Information on individual tribes can be found in
1970 and 1980 reports. In 1980, American <u>Indians</u> were grouped with
Eskimos and Aleuts in some tables on race.

<u>Industry</u>. A classification system for the various types of enter-
prises has been developed by the Census Bureau over the decades. In
most modern censuses, employed persons have been categorized as working within certain <u>industries</u>, as well as in certain occupations.

<u>Institutional population</u>. This category includes persons living in
any type of institution, such as hospitals, nursing homes, group
homes and prisons. Data on this group are often found in tables entitled "households," although this population is not designated as
living in households. In 1950, the term "quasi households" was used
for some types of institutions.

<u>Labor force</u>. This is a term which was put into use early in the
twentieth century by the Census Bureau and has a very specific meaning, as distinguished from "employment." Generally, it includes persons with jobs, whether working or temporarily away from jobs such as
on layoff, and persons looking for and available for work. <u>Labor
force</u> data for 1950 and 1960 include that for persons 14 years and
over; for 1970, for those 14 and 15 and over; and for 1980, for those
16 and over.

<u>Language</u>. There was no question on <u>language</u> in 1950, and in 1960
the question on <u>language</u> was restricted to that of the foreign
born. The 1970 question on this subject was, "What language, other
than English, was spoken in this person's home when he was a child?"
The 1980 questions developed further information: "Does this person
speak a language other than English at home? (If so) What is this
language? And how well does this person speak English?"

<u>Literacy</u>. There is no data on literacy in this volume. Questions
on literacy were asked from 1840 through 1930 but after that were
dropped in favor of a question on years of school completed.

Marital status. The term married includes those married once, re-married, in common-law marriage, and married but separated. Information on the age at first marriage and whether once married has been collected since 1940. In 1970 and 1980, in the case of those married more than once, a question was asked as to how the marriage ended. Although it was the Census which first began to collect vital statistics in the United States, in the middle of the nineteenth century, that function has long since been taken over by other government agencies. A few volumes which appear in this guide, however, do include some statistics on marriages. A better source for such statistics is the volume entitled Marriage and Divorce, one of the four annual Vital Statistics volumes published by the federal government, with information as to the events of marriages as opposed to the marital condition on the census date.

Mexicans. In the 1930 Census, Mexicans were shown as a separate race; in 1940, they were shown as "White"; and in 1950, also as "White" unless "Indian or definitely another race." Beginning in 1960, information on Spanish heritage, Spanish origin, Spanish language, or Spanish surname was collected. In some cases these data were collected only in the five southwestern states of Arizona, California, Colorado, New Mexico and Texas.

Migration/Mobility. As used in this volume, this term refers to lifetime or recent moves. Census questions as to state of residence and state of birth, state of residence 5 or other number of years before the census date, and year moved into present house are included in this category. Some data in this category are shown as state of birth. This term does not refer to births abroad, as that information is shown under the term nativity.

Military/Veterans. Each census for the years 1950 through 1980 includes some question in this area. In 1950, the question was "(If male) did he ever serve in the U.S. Armed Forces during World War II, World War I, or any other time, including present service?" A similar question was asked in 1960 and 1970, still restricted to males, with the addition of the Korean War in 1960 and the Vietnam Conflict in 1970. In 1980, all adults in the sample were asked: "In April 1975, was this person on active duty in the Armed Forces?" and "Is this person a veteran of active-duty military service in the Armed Forces of the United States?" and the period of duty. In addition, information on group quarters includes a category for military barracks.

Minor civil divisions. These are the primary divisions of counties established by state law. The exact definition differs for individual states, and the census volume should always be consulted when this category for a certain state is important.

Nativity. This characteristic is determined by the place of birth. Tables are generally divided into native or foreign born (referred to in this guide as general nativity). Other tables are specific by country of birth. In addition, the 1950, 1960 and 1970 Censuses asked for the place of birth of father and of mother. The 1960 questionnaire also asked, "Is this person's origin or descent Mexican, Puerto Rican, Cuban, Central or South American, Other Spanish, or none of these?" The 1980 Census also asked, "What is this person's ancestry?" Answers to the questions on parents' birthplaces appear in this guide as parental nativity, and under the term foreign stock. Data on Spanish origin appear under "demographic characteristics."

Occupations. Information on occupations of the population has been gathered since early in the nineteenth century. The four censuses in this volume have similar data, with at least one table in each providing very specific data. In 1950 and each successive census, there was at least one publication indexing occupations, either alphabetically or by the Census Bureau's classification system. These indexes were published in time for the enumeration and were developed to provide the enumerators and/or coders with the proper classification for each individual's occupation. It should be noted that distinction must be made between occupation and industry. For example, a carpenter working for a college would fall into an occupational category subsumed under "craftsmen," but within the industry of "education."

Oklahoma Identified Historic Areas (excluding urbanized areas). These are former reservation areas which had legally established boundaries between 1900 and 1907, when Oklahoma became a state. They were dissolved by 1907, but data are provided in the 1980 Census.

Outlying areas. Areas in this group which appear in the 1950-1980 census volumes include Puerto Rico, Panama Canal Zone, the Virgin Islands of the United States, American Samoa, Wake, Midway and other Pacific Islands, Guam and the Trust Territories of the Pacific Islands. For additional information see the pages entitled "States, and Outlying Areas."

Place. This is a concentration of population with a nucleus of residences, regardless of any legally determined boundaries.

Place of work. The 1960 Census began use of a question on place of work which was continued through 1980. The question refers to the geographical location of the working place in relation to the worker's residence. Data show work in or outside the county of residence, in or out of the Standard Metropolitan Statistical Area of residence, or inside or outside the central city. In this guide, information on this subject appears under the category of employment/ unemployment.

Population. The number of inhabitants.

Poverty. By the 1970's the federal government had established an official poverty level, which is now updated annually. Data from the 1970 and 1980 Censuses appear with a calculation as to the relation of income, usually family income, to the poverty level.

Quasi household. This is a term used in the 1950 Census to denote a group of persons living in quarters designated as a dwelling unit, such as a lodging house, hotel, institution, labor camp or military barracks. In 1950, each household had a "head," and the head of the quasi household was the manager, hotelkeeper, or other such designee. After 1950, the term "group quarters" replaced this term.

Race. This demographic characteristic has always been the subject of census inquiry. Much information has been provided on race by age, sex, marital status and by most social and economic characteristics. Although many tables in each census are headed "White" and "nonwhite," the published reports of each census also contain tables with information on each race. There is also one subject report on race in each of the four censuses in this guide. No distinction is made in most tables of this guide as to the amount of detail regarding race.

Rural. The portion of the area which is not urban. Where the definition of urban is important, the appropriate decennial census volume should be consulted.

Sex. This has always been a subject of census inquiry and is always a 100 percent question, never a sample question. Most census data are tabulated by sex, but often the table guides published in the census volumes do not show that. In this guide it is usually indicated.

Spanish heritage, origin, surname. The Census Bureau has been increasing its efforts to develop better data on the Spanish population in recent years. In 1960, some data were developed and published; in 1970 there was a 15 percent sample question on Spanish heritage and also a 5 percent sample question, with different data developed for different states. By 1980, the question on Spanish background was a complete count question. Some additional data has also been gathered for persons of Puerto Rican birth or parentage.

Standard Consolidated Area. This is a group of contiguous Standard Metropolitan Statistical Areas. The term was first used in 1960, when two such areas were designated: the New York City-Northeast New Jersey area and the Chicago-Northwestern Indiana area. By 1980 there were more such areas.

Standard Metropolitan Areas and Standard Metropolitan Statistical Areas. These are terms developed by the Census Bureau to denote populated areas. The first term was used in 1950 and the second term thereafter. Each term has a very specific meaning, and the census definition should be consulted by anyone needing precise data. Generally, these areas are designated when there is a city of 50,000 persons, and the area includes the entire county in which the city is located. Sometimes two or more contiguous counties comprise an area. Each of the political entities in the area is referred to as a "component part." Designation of SMSA's, as they are frequently known, is made not by the Census Bureau but by the Office of Management and Budget in the Office of the President.

State Economic Areas. These are designated areas of states with homogeneous economic and social characteristics. Reference to these areas was most frequent in 1950 and 1960, when there were 509 such areas.

States. There were 48 states in 1950, and 50 by 1960. Data for the District of Columbia are included with that for states.

Territories. In 1950, there were but two remaining jurisdictions in this category which were still to become states: Alaska and Hawaii. Alaska became the 49th state in January 1959, and Hawaii the 50th in August of the same year. Thus each appears as a territory in the 1950 Census, and a state thereafter.

Transportation. Most of the information on this subject refers to travel to work. The question as to how one reaches one's place of work began with the 1960 Census and has been used in the two censuses since. Travel time to work was included in the 1980 Census. Some of the data published on this subject was part of the Census of Housing, which has included a question as to the number of vehicles available at a housing unit. In 1980, a question as to the ability to use public transit was included in the questionnaire.

Unemployment. See Employment.

Unincorporated places. These are areas of densely settled popula-
ion without corporate limits but determined in advance of the enumeration by the Census Bureau in order to develop statistical information.

Unrelated individuals. Persons not living with any relatives. The
term is usually found in tables on households or families. Often,
income is computed for such persons separately, so as not to skew
calculations for family incomes.

Urban. The term is used throughout census publications and is used
in distinction from rural. The population which is not classified
as urban population is classified as rural population. It is important for anyone needing a precise definition to consult the definition in each decennial census. Generally, however, it can be stated
that places of 2,500 or more inhabitants are considered urban.

Urban fringe. See Urbanized area below.

Urbanized area. In 1950 the Census Bureau developed this concept
to indicate a separation of the urban and the rural population. Such
an area consists of a central city or cities and the surrounding area
which is closely settled. The latter is defined as the urban fringe.
By 1980 there were 366 urbanized areas in the United States and 7
more in Puerto Rico. Definitions published in the census reports
should be referred to by anyone needing precise descriptions.

Vital Statistics. The collection of data on vital events (births,
marriages, divorces and deaths) began with the Census as early as
1850, but the function has long since been turned over to other
U.S. government agencies. Whereas the census is an enumeration of
the population as of a certain date, April 1st in modern times, vital
statistics data result from counts of vital events. The census is
mandated by the Constitution as a federal function, but the recording
of vital events is generally considered a state function.

The federal government has, however, for over a century collected and
published vital statistics information. Standard forms for recording
births, marriages and deaths are generally used nationwide, and
data are published annually in four Vital Statistics volumes by
the Department of Health and Human Services.

Some questions in recent censuses do elicit some <u>vital statistics</u> data such as the number of times married and the <u>number of children</u> born to a woman. In this guide, such information is shown under the titles of <u>marital status</u> and <u>fertility</u>, but in a few instances data are shown under the term <u>vital statistics</u>.

<u>Wage or salary income or worker</u>. A term applied to one whose earnings come from employment by others. <u>Wage and salary income</u> includes money earnings for work performed, whether wages, salary, pay from Armed Forces, commissions, tips, piece-rate payments or cash bonuses.

STATES AND OUTLYING AREAS IN 1950-1980 CENSUS VOLUMES

STATES

The following were states in the Union prior to 1950 and thus appear in 1950-1980 Census volumes as such, together with the District of Columbia:

Alabama	Maine	Ohio
Arizona	Maryland	Oklahoma
Arkansas	Massachusetts	Oregon
California	Michigan	Pennsylvania
Colorado	Minnesota	Rhode Island
Connecticut	Mississippi	South Carolina
Delaware	Missouri	South Dakota
District of Columbia	Montana	Tennessee
Florida	Nebraska	Texas
Georgia	Nevada	Utah
Idaho	New Hampshire	Vermont
Illinois	New Jersey	Virginia
Indiana	New Mexico	Washington
Iowa	New York	West Virginia
Kansas	North Carolina	Wisconsin
Kentucky	North Dakota	Wyoming
Louisiana		

TERRITORIES WHICH SUBSEQUENTLY BECAME STATES

Territory	Organized as Territory	Appears as Territory in Censuses of	Admitted as State
Alaska	1912	1900, 1910, 1920, 1930, 1940, 1950	1959. See notes on next page
Hawaii	1900	1900, 1910, 1920, 1930, 1940, 1950	1959. See notes on next page

States and Outlying Areas

Alaska

Alaska was purchased from the Russion government in 1867. There had been enumerations of
the population between 1818 and that time.
Alaska was first enumerated for the U.S.Census
in 1880, and that census resulted in two reports: Alaska: Its Population and Resources
and The Seal Islands of Alaska. In 1890, as
a result of that census, another major volume
was published on Alaska, entitled Report on
Population and Resources of Alaska. After
1890, Alaska continued to be enumerated in
each decennial census, but no separate volume
was published. Alaska was organized as a territory in 1912, and admitted as a state in
1959, and thus appears as a state in the Censuses of 1960, 1970 and 1980.

American Samoa

This group of Pacific Ocean Islands became a
U.S. possession upon the signing of a conven-
tion with Great Britain and Germany in Decem-
ber, 1899. All islands were placed under the
authority of the Secretary of the Navy, and
the naval governors took the first censuses in
1900 and 1912. Since 1920, American Samoa has
been enumerated as a regular part of each decennial U.S. census.

Guam

Guam became a U.S. possession folowing the
treaty signed with Spain in 1898 at the con-
clusion of the Spanish-American War. The
naval governors were responsible for the census, the first of which was taken in 1901 and
the second in 1910. Since 1920, Guam has been
enumerated as a regular part of each decennial
U.S. Census.

Hawaii

A census was taken as early as 1832 by the
Hawaiian government, and successive censuses
were taken through 1896. Hawaii became a U.S.
possession in 1898, and was organized as a
territory in 1900. Hawaii was enumerated as a
regular part of the U.S. census each decade
from 1900 through 1950. It was admitted as a
state in 1959, and enumerated as a state since
the 1960 Census.

States and Outlying Areas

Panama Canal Zone.	The Panama Canal Zone came under U.S. sovereignty in 1903, and the first census was taken in 1912 by the Isthmian Canal Commission. The Canal Zone was thereafter enumerated as part of the U.S. Census each decade from 1920 through 1970. In 1977, the United States and the Republic of Panama agreed upon two treaties which would provide for the takeover of the Canal Zone by the Republic in 1999. The treaties were ratified by the U.S. Senate in 1978, and the Canal Zone was not enumerated in the 1980 Census.
Puerto Rico	Like other islands, Puerto Rico was ceded to the U.S. by Spain in 1898 at the close of the Spanish-American War. The War Department took a census in 1899, and thereafter Puerto Rico was enumerated as a part of the regular U.S. Census. Prior to the 1930 Census, the Census Bureau spelled the name as Porto Rico. For several decades, the reports on the enumeration have been published in both English and Spanish. Puerto Rico is a self-governing Commonwealth, with a population of about two million United States citizens.
Trust Territory of the Pacific Islands including the Mariana Islands	The U.S. Trust Territory of the Pacific Islands includes an area of over 3 million square miles, with over 2000 islands, only about one hundred of them inhabited. The Carolines, the Marshalls, and the Marianas are three of the major groups of islands. The United Nations placed these islands under the United States as a Trust Territory following World War II. THe Carolines and the Marshalls have been under the jurisdiction of the Interior Department since 1951, but the people of the Marianas voted in 1975 to become a U.S. Commonwealth, and in 1977 the Congress and the President approved their Constitution which provides for island control of domestic affairs and U.S. control of defense and foreign affairs.
U.S. Virgin Islands	These Caribbean Islands, formerly known as the Danish West Indies, were purchased from Denmark

in 1917. The three main islands are St.Thomas, St.Croix and St.John, but there are some 65 small islands in the group, many uninhabited The population had been enumerated several times by the Danish government between 1838 and 1911. In 1917, a special census was taken under the supervision of the U.S. Census Bureau, and since 1920 the population has been enumerated as a regular part of the U.S. Census.

GENERAL NOTE

Volume I of the 1940 Census provides excellent histories, together with both then current and historic population counts for each of the territories then under U.S. sovereignty: Alaska, Amaerican Samoa, Guam, Hawaii, Panama Canal Zone, Puerto Rico and the U.S. Virgin Islands.

SUBJECTS OF QUESTIONNAIRE ITEMS ON 1950-1980 DECENNIAL CENSUSES

SUBJECT	1950	1960	1970	1980
Demographic Characteristics				
Age	x	x	x	x
Race or color	x	x	x	x
American Indian tribe	x		x	x
Spanish origin, surname or heritage			x*	x
Marital status	x	x	x	x
Household relationship	x	x	x	x
Social and Economic Characteristics				
Citizenship	x	x**	xs	xs
Disabilities			xs	xs
Education	xs	xs	xs	xs
Employment/unemployment	x	xs	xs	xs
Farmers/farms	x	xsh	xh	
Immigration	x	xs	xs	xs
Income	xs	xs	xs	xs
Industry	x	xs	xs	xs
Language	xs	xs	xs	xs
Migration/mobility	xs	xs	xs	xs
Military/veterans	xs	xs	xs	xs
Nativity	x	xs	xs	xs
Occupation	x	xs	xs	xs
Transportation		xs	xs	xs

---

x   Item on population census questionnaire
h   Item on housing census questionnaire
s   Item asked only of sample population
*   Item asked only in 5 southwestern states
** Item asked only in New York City and Puerto Rico and on separate
     questionnaire used for Americans abroad

BIBLIOGRAPHY

BUREAU OF THE CENSUS PUBLICATIONS

All decennial censuses prior to 1950 were catalogued by Henry J. Dubester in the volume listed below. He completed that work in 1950 as head of the Census Library Project, a joint effort of the Library of Congress and the Bureau of the Census. His system of numerical annotation, referred to by librarians as "Dubester Numbers," was used to organize the two previous volumes of this series of guides. There are no such numbers for the 1950-1980 census publications, and they are referred to in this guide by their other publication designations, such as volume and part numbers.

CATALOGS

1950

Dubester, Henry J.   Catalog of U.S. Census Publications, 1790-1945. U.S. Department of Commerce, Bureau of the Census and U.S. Library of Congress, Reference Department. Census Library Project. Washington, DC: Government Printing Office. x, 320 pages.

1974

U.S. Department of Commerce, Social and Economic Statistics Administration, Bureau of the Census. Bureau of the Census Catalog of Publications, 1790-1972. Washington, DC: Government Printing Office. x, 320, 591 pages.

This volume includes the entire text of the 1790-1945 Dubester volume above, with its pages clearly distinguishable at the front, printed on yellow paper and separately numbered. It also includes a list of publications from the 1960 Census. As many of the reports of the 1970 Census had not been published in 1972, this newer catalog does not contain a complete list of census volumes for 1970, but only for 1950 and 1960. So far as I can determine, the Census Bureau has never published a separate catalog listing its published materials from the 1970 Census, nor from the 1980 Census, in a single reference source.

1979

U.S. Department of Commerce, Bureau of the Census. 1980 Census of Population and Housing: Tentative Publication and Computer Tape Program. Washington, DC: Department of Commerce, Bureau of the Census. 1979. 6 pages.

Bibliography

This valuable brief foldout publication contains a list of all the contemplated publications of both the population and housing censuses, together with a final list of the subject items, both 100 percent and sample, used in the enumeration.

1986

U.S. Department of Commerce, Bureau of the Census. Census Catalog and Guide: 1986. Washington, DC: Government Printing Office. 472 pages.

1987

U.S. Department of Commerce, Bureau of the Census. Census Catalog and Guide: 1987. Washington, DC: Government Printing Office. 459 pages.

GUIDES AND OTHER RESOURCE MATERIALS

Bureau of the Census Library. Decennial Censuses Indexes: 1900-180. Washington, DC: Bureau of the Census. n.d., c. 1982. 2 pages processed.

Bureau of the Census Library. United States Census Publications in Microform. Washington, DC: Bureau of the Census, 1984. 4 pages processed.

Department of Commerce, Bureau of the Census. Conference on Census Undercount: Proceedings. Washington, DC: Government Printing Office. 1980. 244 pages.

Kaplan, Charles P., and Van Valey, Thomas S. Census '80: Continuing the Factfinder Tradition. U.S. Department of Commerce, Bureau of the Census. Washington, DC: Government Printing Office. 1980. xviii, 490 pages.

Shryock, Henry S., Jacob S. Siegel, and Associates. Methods and Materials of Demography. U.S. Department of Commerce, Bureau of the Census. Washington, DC: Government Printing Office. 1971. 2 volumes. v.1 xvi, 369, 20 pages; v.2 xv, 888, 20 pages.

U.S. Department of Commerce, Bureau of the Census. Twenty Censuses: Population and Housing Questions, 1790-1980. Washington, DC: Government Printing Office. 1978. iv, 91 pages.

314

Bibliography

U.S. Department of Commerce, Social and Economic Statistics in Administration, Bureau of the Census. <u>Population and Housing Inquiries in U.S. Decennial Censuses, 1790-1970</u>. Working Paper 39. Washington, DC: Department of Commerce, 1973. iv, 179 pages.

MICROFORM COLLECTIONS AND GUIDES THERETO

Congressional Information Service., Inc.
<u>American Statistics Index</u>. 1974 retrospective, and annual indexes 1974-1986. Bethesda, Maryland: Congressional Information Service, Inc. 1975 et seq.

<u>Guide to 1980 U.S. Decennial Census Publications</u>. <u>Index and Abstracts</u>. 2 vol. 1986.

<u>American Statistics Index</u>. Microfiche collection. 1974-1986.

Research Publications, Inc. Woodbridge, Connecticut.
<u>Bibliography and Reel Index: A Guide to the Microfilm Edition of the United States Decennial Census Publications, 1790-1970</u>. 1975.

<u>Microfilm Edition of the United States Decennial Census Publications, 1790-1970</u>. Roll film. 1975.

INDEXES, ATLASES AND GUIDES PUBLISHED BY OTHER PUBLISHERS

Andriot, John L., compiler and editor. <u>Township Atlas of the United States</u>. McLean, Virginia: Andriot Associates, 1979.

Farrington, Polly-Alida. <u>Subject Index to the 1980 Census of Population and Housing</u>. Clifton Park, New York: Specialized Information Products. 1985. 211 pages.

Martis, Kenneth C., and Ruth Anderson Rowles. <u>The Historical Atlas of United States Congressional Districts, 1789-1983</u>. New York and London: The Free Press, 1982. 302 pages.

Poole, Mary Elizabeth. <u>Documents Office Classification to 1966</u>, Third Edition. Ann Arbor, Michigan: Xerox Education Division, University Microfilms Library Services. 1967. Processed.

Schulze, Suzanne. <u>A Century of the Colorado Census</u>. Greeley, Colorado: The University of Northern Colorado, Michener Library, 1976. Revised with microform collection, 1977.

Bibliography

-----. Population Information in Nineteenth Century Census Volumes. Phoenix, Arizona: The Oryx Press, 1983.

-----. Population Information in Twentieth Century Census Volumes: 1900-1940. Phoenix, Arizona: The Oryx Press, 1985.

University of Texas, Population Research Center. International Population Bibliography. Vol. 4 North America. Austin, Texas: University of Texas Bureau of Business Research, 1966, and 1974 Addendum.

AVAILABILITY OF CENSUS MATERIALS

The purpose of this volume, as was that of the two earlier ones in the set, is to make access to census materials easier. A more basic purpose is to call attention to the enormous amount of information available through the United States decennial censuses.

Census volumes are available through the Depository Library system established by Congress in the nineteenth century. They are now also available through the Bureau of the Census State Data Centers, which have been established in most, if not all, states. In addition, assistance in the use of the census is always available from the Bureau of the Census Regional Center Data Users Service.

Population census materials are also available from commercial publishers in microform. Those from the 1950, 1960 and 1970 Censuses are available on roll microfilm from Research Publications, Inc. Those from the 1980 Census, and some from the 1970 Census, are available from Congressional Information Service through its American Statistics Index microfiche. Further information on these collections is included in the bibliography.

Below are spaces for librarians to note the address, telephone and names of contact person at their Regional Depository Library, their Census Bureau State Data Center and their closest Bureau of the Census Data Users Service Regional Center. Although the latter two, established by the Bureau of the Census to assist users of census material, are usually extremely accomodating, they do not ordinarily hold census historic collections, both having been established about 1980. They often are, however, knowledgeable about census collections in their areas of service. Regional Depository Libraries, which are required to retain their U.S. depository collections, often do have extensive historical census volumes. It is their obligation to give access to other depository libraries in their area.

Regional Depository Library

Address

Phone

Contact persons

State Data Center

Address

Phone

Contact persons

Bureau of the Census, Census Data Users Service Regional Center

Address

Phone

Contact persons

Below are spaces to list information about other libraries holding census materials within the borrowing area. Some libraries are reluctant to lend census volumes, but many would be willing to make copies of individual tables. Users of this guide should feel free to make copies of its pages so that they may more readily make use of census library materials.

Other Libraries Holding 1950-1980 Census Volumes

Library A

Address

Phone

Contact Person

Library B

Address

Phone

Contact Person

Suzanne Schulze is Archives Librarian and Professor of Library Science at the University of Northern Colorado in Greeley. She is currently editor of The Colorado Archivist. Her publications include two earlier ones, Population Information in Nineteenth Century Census Volumes and Population Information in Twentieth Century Census Volumes: 1900-1940, both published by The Oryx Press. With this latest volume she has completed reference guides for the twenty decennial censuses from 1790 through 1980.

Guide to Volumes 1980

1980

	Vol I Ch A Part 1	Parts 2–58 States	Ch B Part 1	Parts 2–58 States	Ch C Part 1	Parts 2–58 States	Ch D Part 1	Parts 2–55 States	Vol II Part 1	Part 2	Part 4	Part 6	Part 7	Part 8	Part 9	Report 1	Report 2	Report 3	Report 4	Report 5	Report 6
Demographic Characteristics																					
Aggregate population	●	●	●	●	●	●	●	●	●	●	●		●	●	●	●	●	●	●	●	●
Age			●	●	●	●	●	●	●	●	●			●	●	●					●
Race			●	●	●	●	●	●	●	●	●	●	●	●	●			●		●	
Spanish origin			●	●	●	●	●	●	●	●	●	●	●	●	●					●	
Sex			●	●	●	●	●	●	●	●	●	●	●	●	●						●
Marital status			●	●	●	●	●	●	●	●	●			●							
Social and Economic Characteristics																					
Citizenship					●	●	●	●	●												
Disabilities					●	●					●										
Education					●	●	●	●	●	●	●		●	●	●						
Employment/unemployment					●	●	●	●	●		●	●	●	●	●						
Families			●	●	●	●	●	●	●		●			●	●						
Farmers/farms														●							
Fertility			●	●	●	●	●	●	●					●							
Households			●	●	●	●	●	●	●	●	●			●	●		●		●	●	●
Housing									●					●	●					●	
Immigration					●	●	●	●	●												
Income					●	●	●	●	●	●	●	●	●	●	●						
Industry					●	●	●	●	●	●		●	●	●							
Institutional population			●	●	●	●		●		●											
Labor force					●	●	●	●	●	●	●		●	●							
Language					●	●	●	●	●												
Migration/mobility					●	●	●	●	●	●	●			●							
Military/veterans					●	●	●			●	●	●	●								
Nativity					●	●	●	●			●										
Occupations					●	●	●	●	●	●	●	●	●	●	●						
Poverty					●	●	●	●	●					●	●						
Transportation					●	●	●	●				●		●							
Apportionment, Geography																					
Apportionment	●																				
Geography	●	●	●	●	●	●			●	●	●	●		●						●	
Vital Statistics																					